woodworking

TOOLS

and how to use them

woodworking
TOOLS
and how to use them

An abridgement of
Tools and How to Use Them for Woodworking
and Metal Working

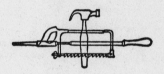

written and illustrated with 300
drawings by ALFRED P. MORGAN

GRAMERCY PUBLISHING COMPANY

New York

CONTENTS

WOODWORKING
TOOLS

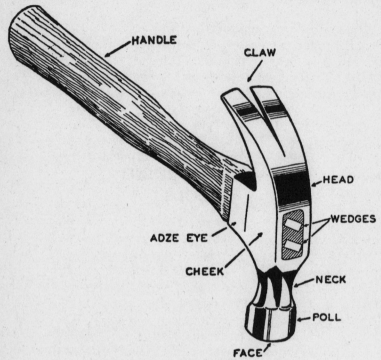

HANDLE

CLAW

HEAD

WEDGES

ADZE EYE

CHEEK

NECK

POLL

FACE

THE COMMON CLAW HAMMER FOR DRIVING
AND PULLING NAILS

1   The Technique of Using Tools; Interesting Facts about the Nail Hammer and Nails

CIVILIZATION'S progress is told in the story of its tools. Primitive man used a few clumsy tools made of stone. We are fortunate in the possession of ingenious and efficient implements of fine steel which extend the force and abilities of our hands many thousandfold. Without our hammers, chisels, drills, saws, dies, wrenches, etc., our living standards would be those of the cave-man or Pueblo Indian.

Human beings are blessed with ten strong, amazingly dextrous fingers and a world filled with raw materials from which can be fashioned almost anything that may be desired. But fingers alone cannot cut wood and metal and stone. Not much progress can be made in driving a nail with the fist. It is obvious that hands, even though they are guided by an ingenious brain, must have tools to accomplish much.

Anyone possessed of ordinary coordination can easily learn to handle tools efficiently. It is not difficult to use, or to learn how to use, most of the ordinary tools with skill. Do not be dismayed by the dexterity of a skilled workman. Proper instruction and practice will make you skillful also.

First, you must understand the tools you propose to use, their purposes and limitations; then, the proper way to hold them and apply them to the work.

To get the most out of a tool, we do not, for example, pick up a hammer and merely whack at a nail with it or push a saw back and forth to cut wood. We learn the *technique* of using each tool. Starting right is half the secret. If we start right, we soon acquire skill by practicing. If we start wrong, practice will not bring skill. Striking a blow is not all there is to using a hammer. There can be artistry in its use or in the use of a saw, a wrench, a screw driver, a plane, or in fact of any other tool. The skilled mechanic is skilled in the use of his tools because he knows more about his tools than the novice and has learned the technique of using them. His tools have become extensions of his hands and brain.

You can learn how to use tools properly from a good mechanic and from a good book. Not all mechanics are good teachers.

It helps if you know why a tool is made the way it is and how it does the job it was intended for. How to hold a tool correctly is very important.

Some persons cannot drive a nail straight with the result that sometimes they hit fingers as well as the nail. That is because there is something to be known in order to drive a nail properly, and they do not know that something.

Let us consider first the three tools most commonly used in the household and by woodworkers, viz., hammers, screw drivers, and saws.

The Nail or Claw Hammer **Its Purpose.** The nail or claw hammer is a woodworker's tool which mechanics use principally to drive nails, wedges and dowels. The curved claws are used to pull out nails or rip woodwork apart. If the claws have a pronounced curve, the hammer was designed to be more efficient at pulling nails than ripping woodwork apart. If the claws are only slightly curved the hammer is better adapted to ripping than nail pulling. There is also a semi-ripping pattern of hammer, intended as a happy medium between the best ripper and the best nail puller.

A claw hammer designed for nail pulling is usually part of the tool kit of every household. Here it is used not only to drive and pull nails but often serves a great variety of other purposes ranging from homicide to cracking walnuts. A good mechanic does not put his hammer to quite such diversified use. He does not try to break kindling wood or drive cold chisels with it. He chops kindling wood with a hatchet; he drives punches and cold chisels with a machinist's hammer.

We can divide nail hammers into two other classifications: those sold in the dime stores to the neophyte woodworker and would-be interior decorator and the hammers which mechanics use.

The Specifications of a Good Hammer. The dime store hammer has a cast head, whose face is not accurately ground.

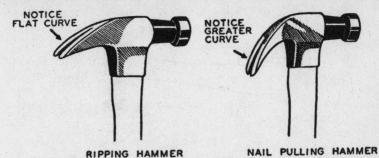

RIPPING HAMMER   NAIL PULLING HAMMER

Ripping Hammer and Nail-Pulling Hammer

The flat curvature of its claws makes the ripping hammer more efficient for pulling apart woodwork than for drawing out nails.

It soon chips and loses its shape. It slips off the heads of nails. It is an ideal tool for driving nails crooked and hammering fingers.

Mechanics' nail hammers may be obtained from any tool and hardware supplier. The head of a first-class hammer is not cast. It is drop forged from tough alloy steel and is tempered and heat treated so that it is twice as strong as ordinary steel. A cast head is made by pouring white hot steel into a sand mold. A drop-forged head is made by hammering red-hot steel into a steel die. A cast head is brittle; a drop-forged head is really tough.

The head of a first-class hammer is accurately ground to shape. The face is usually ground smooth and slightly beveled at the edge to prevent chipping, although carpenters sometimes use a hammer having a face roughened by cross checkering which is often employed for nailing together the frame of a building. The smooth-faced, slightly convex or "bell-face" hammer is the most generally useful. A hammer handle is tough, seasoned, straight-grained hickory shaped to fit the hand at one end and tapered toward the head so as to give the hammer its "spring." An important quality of a hammer handle is spring which gives the mechanic better control of the tool and eases the strain on his muscles. You can best appreciate this by driving a few nails with a hammer head fitted with a solid metal handle. Not only will it not feel right, but your muscles will soon be shocked and tired. That end of the hickory handle which is fitted into a hammer head is expanded into the tapered eye usually by one wooden wedge and two metal wedges so that it cannot

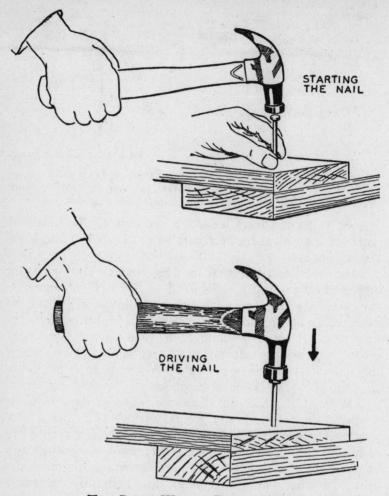

The Right Way to Drive a Nail

Grasp nail near its point with thumb and forefinger. Place point on work and strike head one or two light blows with hammer to start point into the wood. Then get your fingers out of the way and drive nail in with positive firm blows. The instant the hammer strikes the nail, the direction of its motion should be parallel to the axis of the nail.

come off easily.

Hammer Sizes. The size of a nail hammer is the weight of the head in ounces ranging from 5 oz. to 28 oz. The common sizes are 10 oz., 12 oz., 14 oz., 16 oz. and 20 oz. The lighter hammers are used for driving small nails. The heaviest is used for driving large nails into soft wood or ordinary nails into hard wood. When the hammer used is too light for the job it will cause a nail to bend. It should be so heavy that a large nail can be driven in completely with five blows. A 16 oz. hammer is a good choice for general use.

The Plain-Face and Bell-Face. A smooth-face nail hammer may have either a bell face or a plain face. The face is the part of the hammer head which strikes against the nail. On a bell-face hammer it is slightly more convex than on a plain-face hammer. The novice cannot drive nails straight as easily with a bell-face hammer as with a plain-face hammer. However, there is a good reason why a bell-face hammer is frequently used. With it, an experienced mechanic can drive a nail flush, or even slightly below the surface of the work, without leaving any hammer marks on the wood.

How to Use a Claw Hammer A great many people who own cast-iron hammers and who think they know how to drive nails should read the rest of this chapter carefully.

Unless you are a confirmed south-paw hold the hammer in your *right* hand. Grasp the handle firmly with the end practically flush with the lower edge of the palm. Grasp the nail near its point with the thumb and forefinger of the other hand. Place the point of the nail on the work at the exact spot where it is to be driven. Unless the nail is to be purposely driven at an angle it should be *perpendicular* to the surface of the work. Rest the face of the hammer at its center on the head of the nail, raise the hammer slightly and give the nail one or two light taps to start the nail and fix your aim. Then get your fingers out of the way and drive the nail in as far as you want it to go. The wrist and arm motion used in driving the nail depends upon the power of the blows required. Small nails require light blows which are struck almost entirely with a wrist motion. Slightly heavier, or medium blows are struck with both a wrist and a forearm motion. The heavy blows required to drive a large nail come from the wrist, forearm and shoulder. Do not attack a nail viciously. On the other hand, do not be timid. Nails are properly driven with a few positive, firm blows and not with either a pile-driving whack or a series of light taps. Always strike the nail with the center of the hammer face. Do not strike with the side or cheek. Dirt or grease on the hammer face will cause it to slip on the nail. Therefore keep the face clean.

Sometimes the grain of the wood, a knot or a hidden obstruction will cause a nail to bend or go in crooked. Usually it is the fault of the workman.

When a nail is going in straight, strike so that when the hammer hits the head of the nail, the nail is perpendicular to the hammer face. Striking the nail with the face at a slight angle will force the head of the nail forward, sidewise or back depending upon the angle. This is the trick used to straighten up a nail which is not going in the right direction. Slightly changing the angle of the hammer face to the nail is one of the controls.

If a nail bends when it is driven, draw it out and throw it away. Start another in its place. If the second nail also bends, investigation is called for. If the nail appears to be striking a knot, a hidden nail or other metal, it will be necessary to withdraw it. Drive a new nail in a new place. Or drill a small hole through the obstruction and try again.

Using the Bell-Face Hammer. As already mentioned, the head of a nail can be driven slightly below a wooden surface without leaving any hammer marks on the surface by using a bell-face hammer. It is necessary for the face of the hammer to be parallel to the surface of the wood and for the head of the nail to be in the center of the face when it is struck.

Ripping Hammers. Nail hammers are made with two types of claws. One is designed for pulling nails, the other for ripping woodwork apart. Claws designed for nail pulling are more curved than ripping claws. The flat, only slightly curved, claw of a ripping hammer is designed to slip under the edges of the boards and timbers and pry them apart.

Nail Sets. In fine work where the nail head must not show or must be inconspicuous, it is driven well below the surface with a nail set. The hole in the wood over the nail head can then be filled flush with the surface with putty, plastic wood or sawdust mixed with glue. The slender, small headed nails, called finishing nails, are usually set below the

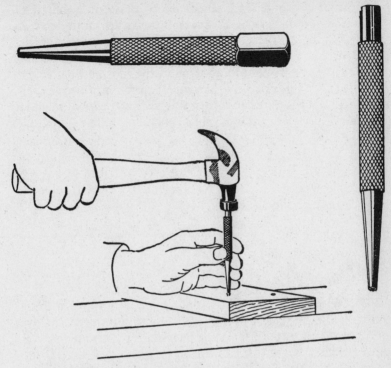

A Nail Set is Used to Drive the Head of a Finishing Nail Below the Surface of the Work

surface. A nail set is used for this purpose.

Nail sets are made in several sizes, usually 1/32″, 2/32″ and 4/32″, the size being indicated by the diameter of the small end of the tapered shank. Notice that the end of a nail set is often "cupped" or hollowed. This helps prevent it from "walking" or slipping on the nail. Use a nail set of a size which will not enlarge the hole made by the head of the nail. It is rather simple to "set" a nail. Hold the nail set between the thumb and forefinger and press the small end firmly against the head of the nail. Rest the little finger on the work to steady your hand and prevent the nail set from slipping. Drive the nail head about 1/16″ below the surface of the wood with a light tap of the hammer. The resulting hole made by the head of the nail can then be concealed by filling it with putty, plastic wood or a mixture of sawdust and glue.

How to Draw a Nail. In order to pull out a nail with a claw hammer, it is necessary for the head of the nail to be above the surface of the work far enough so that the claws of the hammer can be slipped underneath. The slot between the claws should go around the nail and under the nail head. Then raise the hammer handle until it is nearly vertical. If the nail is short, this will withdraw it from the work. If the nail is long and the hammer handle

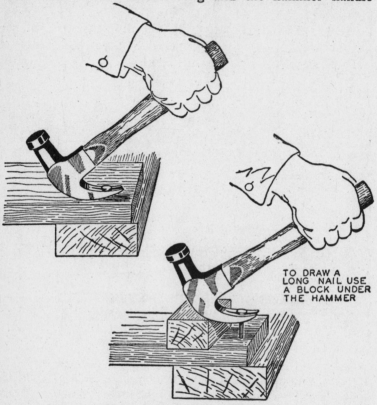

TO DRAW A LONG NAIL USE A BLOCK UNDER THE HAMMER

How to Draw out a Nail

A long nail is drawn by slipping a block of wood between the hammer claws and the work.

is pulled past the vertical position, it will bend the nail, enlarge the hole and mar the work. Moreover when the hammer handle passes the vertical position, most of the leverage is lost and a great deal of force is required to draw out the nail any further.

Here is the simple remedy. Slip a piece of wood between

the hammer head and the work so that the handle is again nearly horizontal and the leverage is increased. This will also apply the pulling force of the claws in the proper direction so that the nail is drawn out without enlarging the hole which it formed when driven into the wood. When long nails, only partially driven into work, must be pulled out, it may be necessary to start the pulling operation with a piece of wood under the hammer head in order to get the proper leverage.

Tack Hammers. Tacks and small nails (brads) can be driven with a light nail hammer but in many instances a tack hammer will prove most efficient.

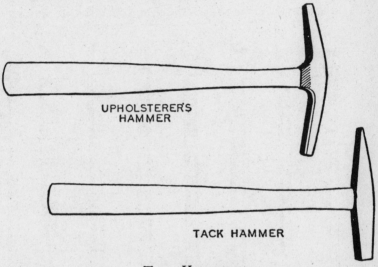

UPHOLSTERER'S HAMMER

TACK HAMMER

TACK HAMMERS

Tacks and small brads can be driven most efficiently with a tack hammer. An upholsterer's hammer is used to tack fabrics on furniture.

Useful Facts About Nails

To the person equipped with a good twenty-five-cent cast-iron hammer "a nail is a nail." If he makes fine distinctions when he buys nails, he specifies "small nails" or "large nails" or perhaps "medium-size nails." In the dictionary a nail is defined as "a slender piece of metal having a head, and used for driving into wood." But a nail is much more significant than either said person's or the dictionary's opinion of it.

It is an important tool used to assemble or hold together a job. There are more than 100 different varieties of nails in common use and this figure does not include the different sizes of each variety. Each has a particular quality which makes it the best to use for certain work.

Nails have been developed from the simple wooden peg of ancient craftsmen. One hundred years ago, they were cut and hammered into shape by hand from wrought iron. Today, nails are produced by automatic machines from wrought iron, steel, copper, brass, bronze, Monel metal and other alloys in hundreds of scientifically designed forms, sizes and shapes. The simple form of the ordinary nail has been modified to meet many specialized requirements. Changing the general proportions and the shape and size

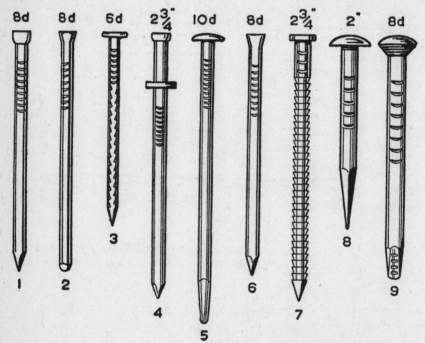

Courtesy American Steel and Wire Company

SPECIAL PURPOSE NAILS

A few of the more than 100 varieties of nails. 1. Common finishing nail. 2. Flooring brad for hardwood. 3. Barbed box nail. 4. Duplex head nail for concrete forms and scaffolds. 5. Clinch nail. 6. Flooring brad. 7. Fetter ring nail. 8. Hinge nail. 9. Boat nail.

of the head and point produces special nails for fastening flooring, shingles, laths, wallboard, baskets, egg crates, fruit boxes, boats, barges, docks, etc., just to name a few examples.

Common Nails. All hardware stores carry in stock common nails and finishing nails. Common nails have flat heads and diamond points. They are the nails which a carpenter uses to fasten together the framework of a building.

Finishing Nails. The nails used to hold trim and finishing woodwork in place are usually driven below the surface

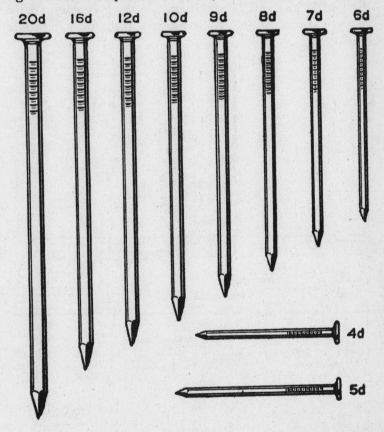

Courtesy American Steel and Wire Company

COMMON NAILS

These are the nails which carpenters use to fasten together the framework of a building. They have flat heads and diamond-shaped points. The full-size sketches can be used to identify 4d to 20d common nails.

of the wood so that the heads do not show. It would be difficult to drive the large flat head of a common nail below the surface, so a carpenter employs finishing nails to accomplish this. Finishing nails have diamond points and brad heads. A brad head is a very small head and can easily be driven into the wood with a nail set.

Brads. These are small diameter diamond-pointed, brad-headed nails which are smaller in diameter than finishing nails. They are used in cabinet making and other fine work.

Wire Nails. Wire nails are diamond-pointed, flat-headed nails which are smaller in diameter than common nails. They are used in light wood which a common nail would probably split.

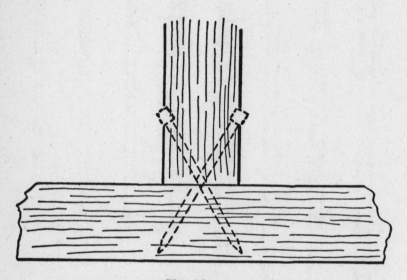

Toe Nailing

It may be necessary to drive nails obliquely in order to fasten the end of one piece of wood to the side of another. This is called toe nailing.

Nail Sizes. Brads and wire nails are sized according to their length and diameter. You can buy little ones only 3/16" in length. The next larger size is 1/4" long. They range from 1/4" by 1/8" to 3" long. The diameter is measured by the American Steel and Wire Gauge and ranges from No. 24 gauge to No. 10 gauge.

Some of the special nails, for example, those used for

brick siding, felt roofing, plasterboard, hinge nails, clout nails, and boat spikes are graded in sizes according to their length in inches. But common nails, finishing nails and a great many others are designated by the penny system.

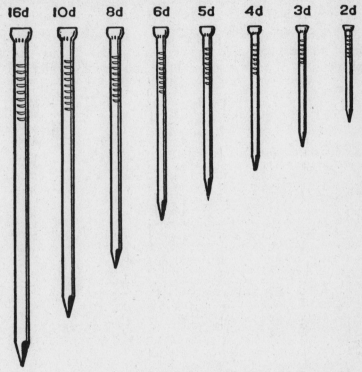

Courtesy American Steel and Wire Company

FINISHING NAILS

Used to hold trim and finishing woodwork in place. The full-size sketches can be used to identify 2d to 16d finishing nails.

The Penny System. This rather clumsy way of designating the sizes of nails originated in England in the dim past and has persisted in the nail industry ever since. No one knows how this curious designation began. One explanation is that two penny, three penny, six penny, etc. nails became known as such from the fact that one hundred cost two pennies, three pennies, four pennies, etc. Both the ancient and modern abbreviation for penny is "d." But whatever the origin of the penny system of designating nails may have been, the fact remains that a 2d nail is 1″ long and each 1 d added increases the length 1/4″ until the 12d size is reached. A 10d nail is 3″ long. The next three sizes larger are the 12d (3 1/4″ long), the 16d (3 1/2″ long), and the 20d (4″ long). After the 20d, come the 30d, 40d, 50d and 60d sizes and these are respectively, 4 1/2″, 5″, 5 1/2″ and 6″ long.

The following tables show the length, diameter, size of head and approximate number to a pound of the various penny sizes of both common nails and finishing nails.

COMMON NAILS *

Size	Length	Diameter (Gauge No.)	Diameter of Head	Approximate Number to a Pound
2 d	1 ″	15	11/64″	830
3 d	1 1/4″	14	13/64″	528
4 d	1 1/2″	12 1/2	1/4 ″	316
5 d	1 3/4″	12 1/2	1/4 ″	271
6 d	2 ″	11 1/2	17/64″	168
7 d	2 1/4″	11 1/2	17/64″	150
8 d	2 1/2″	10 1/4	9/32″	106
9 d	2 3/4″	10 1/4	9/32″	96
10 d	3 ″	9	5/16″	69
12 d	3 1/4″	9	5/16″	63
16 d	3 1/2″	8	11/32″	49
20 d	4 ″	6	13/32″	31
30 d	4 1/2″	5	7/16″	24
40 d	5 ″	4	15/32″	18
50 d	5 1/2″	3	1/2 ″	14
60 d	6 ″	2	17/32″	11

FINISHING NAILS *

Size	Length	Diameter Gauge No.	Diameter of Head Gauge No.	Approximate Number to a Pound
2 d	1 ″	16 1/2	13 1/2	1351
3 d	1 1/4″	15 1/2	12 1/2	807
4 d	1 1/2″	15	12	584
5 d	1 3/4″	15	12	500
6 d	2 ″	13	10	309
8 d	2 1/2″	12 1/2	9 1/2	189
10 d	3 ″	11 1/2	8 1/2	121
16 d	3 1/2″	11	8	90
20 d	4 ″	10	7	62

* The above tables are reprinted from the Catalog of U. S. S. American Nails by courtesy of the American Steel and Wire Company.

Holding Power of Nails. The usefulness of any nail,

regardless of size, depends on its holding power in any given variety of wood. When manufactured, the shank of a nail is therefore roughened near the head to give it greater holding power. Box nails, which must have great holding power when driven into end grain, are roughened or barbed along the entire shank. Some varieties of nails are also coated with an adhesive cement. If you try to knock a fruit box apart by withdrawing the nails, you will probably find that, although the nails are comparatively small, they have great holding power. It is hard to break them loose from the grip of the wood fibers. That is because they are both barbed and cement coated.

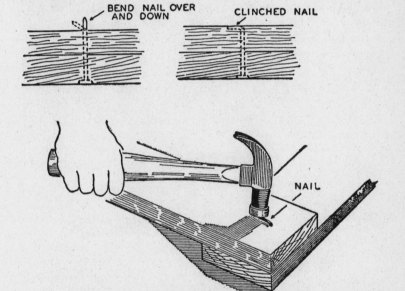

CLINCHED NAILS

Nails are frequently clinched to give them greater holding power. The nail must be long enough to completely penetrate the wood so that the point protrudes. The point is then bent over in line with the grain of the wood and hammered down between the wood fibers. If bent across grain, the point is hammered down until it crushes the fibers. Clinching must be done with care to avoid splitting the wood. The work should rest on a solid surface.

The holding power of a nail is dependent on the closeness of the fibers of the wood into which it is driven. A nail has greater holding power when driven into heavy woods than it has in light woods. Green wood, or wood which is not well seasoned, has a higher holding power than dry wood. If a nail is driven into green wood, its holding power decreases as the wood seasons and dries out.

A nail must be properly selected for the work it is to do so that there is no chance for it to split the wood or unnecessarily distort the fibers. The type of nail that distorts the fibers of the wood the least will have the greatest holding power. The tendency of a nail to split the wood into which it is driven is determined by the shape of the point and the diameter of the nail in relation to the thickness and variety of the wood. A large nail will split a thin or narrow piece of wood. Very sharp points and long diamond points on nails are likely to split hard dense woods. For that reason, a skilled woodworker sometimes uses a file to blunt the point of a nail which he intends to drive into hard wood. Light weight and soft woods which have little tendency to split can be advantageously fastened with sharp pointed nails, somewhat greater holding power being thus secured.

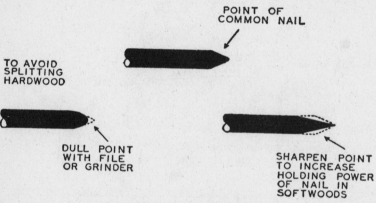

POINT OF COMMON NAIL

TO AVOID SPLITTING HARDWOOD

DULL POINT WITH FILE OR GRINDER

SHARPEN POINT TO INCREASE HOLDING POWER OF NAIL IN SOFTWOODS

A Woodworker's Trick

The common nail has a moderately sharp point with short angles and consequently might be termed an all around nail. It results in only a moderate amount of splitting. Its holding power in soft woods can sometimes be improved by filing the point sharper and its tendency to split hard woods can be reduced by filing the point blunt.

New Handles for Hammers. Well-seasoned hickory makes the best hammer handles. Some mechanics prefer to make their own handles for hammers, hatchets and axes.

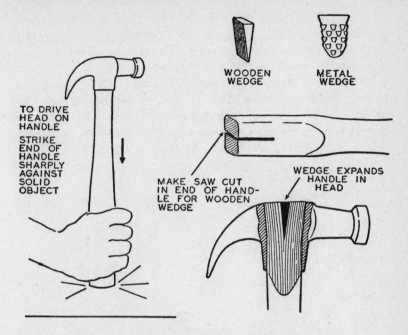

TO DRIVE HEAD ON HANDLE

STRIKE END OF HANDLE SHARPLY AGAINST SOLID OBJECT

WOODEN WEDGE

METAL WEDGE

MAKE SAW CUT IN END OF HANDLE FOR WOODEN WEDGE

WEDGE EXPANDS HANDLE IN HEAD

FITTING A HAMMER WITH A NEW HANDLE

But hardware stores carry machine-made hickory handles in stock so that when a hammer handle breaks it is not difficult to obtain a new one.

That portion of the broken handle which remains in the hammer head must be knocked out. This is not always easy because the end is expanded by the wedges so that it fits the head very tightly. Drilling into the end of the handle with a 3/16″ to 5/16″ diameter twist drill to remove as much wood as possible and then splitting out small pieces will usually remove the old handle.

It may be necessary to scrape or pare the end of a new handle slightly before it will go into the head. This can be done with a knife, chisel, or wood rasp. The handle must fit *very tightly* in the head. The small end of the handle should be inserted in the adze eye, or opening in the head, and the opposite end of the handle struck sharply against the bench top or other solid surface until the handle is in place. Then the end of the handle is expanded in the hammer head by the insertion of wedges so that the head cannot fly off. A hammer with a head which is loose upon the handle is a very dangerous tool. From one to three wedges are generally used. The wedge in the original handle is usually wood, either maple or hickory. Metal wedges of various sizes can be purchased at any hardware store.

When a wooden wedge is used, a saw cut about as long as the wedge should be made with a fine saw into the end of the handle before it is inserted in the head. The wedge is driven into this slot. Of course no wedge should be driven in until the head is on the handle as far as it should go.

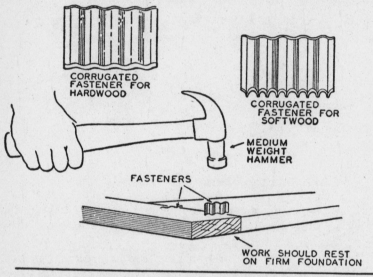

CORRUGATED FASTENER FOR HARDWOOD

CORRUGATED FASTENER FOR SOFTWOOD

MEDIUM WEIGHT HAMMER

FASTENERS

WORK SHOULD REST ON FIRM FOUNDATION

CORRUGATED FASTENERS OR WIGGLE NAILS ARE USED TO FASTEN WOOD SURFACES SIDE BY SIDE

Corrugated Fasteners. These useful devices, often called "wiggle-nails" are used for holding two wood surfaces together side by side. They can be used in making window screens, screen doors, window frames, flower boxes, etc., and for tightening up loose joints or cracks in woodwork. They are made with both a plain and a saw edge. The corrugated fastener with a plain edge is used for hard woods. The saw edge fastener is for the soft woods.

There is a trick in driving a wiggle-nail. It is to use a medium weight hammer and strike light blows which are evenly distributed over the outside edge. It is essential that the work which is being fastened together rest on something solid while the fastener is driven in.

Ripping Bars. Of course a ripping bar is not a hammer, but since it is used, like a hammer, to pull out nails and rip woodwork apart, it is included in this chapter.

There are several varieties of ripping bars. The most common type is the goose-neck pattern. It is drop forged from high grade hexagon tool steel and will not easily bend or break. The goose-neck has two claws like the curved claws of a hammer and is an efficient nail-puller. The chisel-pointed end can be forced into cracks to pry and rip in the same manner that a crow-bar can. A ripping bar is a very useful tool for opening heavy crates and cases and for demolition or wrecking work.

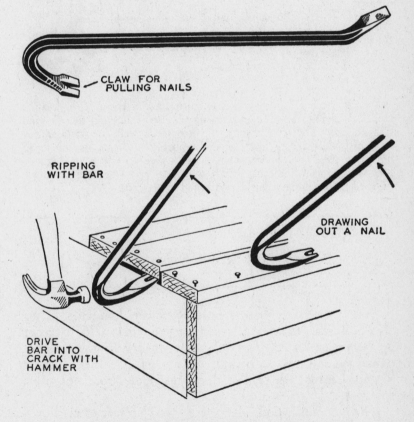

CLAW FOR PULLING NAILS

RIPPING WITH BAR

DRAWING OUT A NAIL

DRIVE BAR INTO CRACK WITH HAMMER

THE RIPPING BAR FOR RIPPING WOODWORK APART AND PULLING NAILS

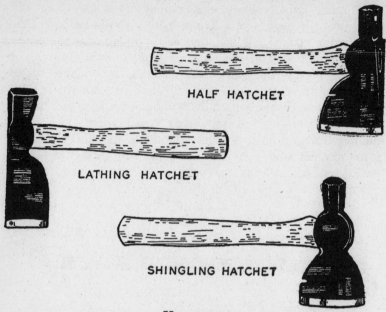

HALF HATCHET

LATHING HATCHET

SHINGLING HATCHET

HATCHETS

Special hatchets are made for shingling and lathing. The head is used for driving nails and the cutting edge for trimming shingles and laths to size. The type called a half hatchet is used by carpenters for roughing which means making cuts requiring neither a smooth finish nor exact size. A half hatchet will often save time in removing surplus stock from a piece of lumber which, after being brought to approximate size, is then finished with a plane or chisel.

2   Screws and Screw Drivers

SCREWS have much greater holding power than nails. They also have the further advantage that work held together by them is easily taken apart and put together again without damaging the pieces. Screws are not used to the exclusion of nails because they are more expensive and take more time to drive.

The common wood screws are made of soft steel and of brass. Steel screws are usually called iron screws. The flathead iron screws generally have a bright finish but are also

plated with nickel, brass, cadmium or (galvanized) zinc.
Round-head iron screws are blued or nickeled.

A screw driver is used primarily for tightening or loosening slotted screws. It is a tool which is often abused in the
hands of a non-mechanic. It is difficult to convince some
people that a screw driver is not a handy combination of
small crow-bar, chisel and can opener. Misusing a screw
driver usually spoils it for driving screws.

All screw drivers are somewhat alike in general appearance but their sizes and shapes vary in design and construction according to work for which they were intended. For
example, opticians' and watchmakers' screw drivers which
are used for fine precision work are small in size and are
turned with the tips of the thumb and forefinger. But heavy,
square-shanked machinists' screw drivers are ruggedly made
and are often turned with a wrench in order to apply extra
force.

STUBBY SCREW DRIVER

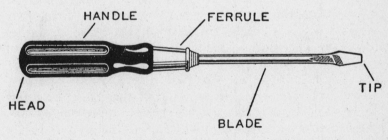

SCREW DRIVERS

As in most things, there is an art in the apparently simple
operation of driving a screw or removing one already in
place. If improperly used, a screw driver may slip and
damage the work or "chew up" the slot in the head of the
screw. Needless to say, a screw with a damaged slot is

usually very difficult to drive in or take out. Incidentally, if you damage the slot in a screw, take it out and throw it away. Do not use it again; replace it with a new one.

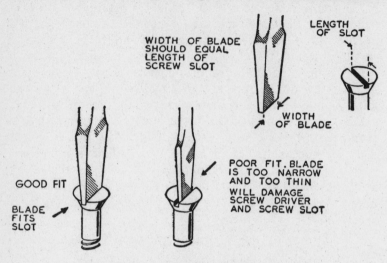

THE TIP OF A SCREW DRIVER SHOULD
FIT THE SCREW SLOT

Screw Driver Sizes. Screw drivers are made in many different sizes and styles. A mechanic always has several sizes. At least two or three sizes should be in every household tool kit. The size of a screw driver is indicated by the length of the blade. A 4-inch screw driver has a blade four inches long; a 6-inch screw driver has a blade six inches long, etc. The width of the blade also varies. A blade with a narrow tip is intended for small screws. If it has a wide tip, it is meant for large screws. There is no all-purpose screw driver; a screw driver must fit the job. The screw drivers used by a machinist are larger and more rugged than those used by a carpenter. Carpenters' screw drivers are larger than those generally employed by an instrument maker.

Screw Drivers in a Tool Kit. Too much emphasis cannot be placed upon the fact that the *tip of a screw driver blade* should fit the screw slot. In order to drive screws of several different sizes, it is necessary to employ several sizes of screw drivers. The thickness of the blade should fit snugly in the screw slot and the width of the blade should be about the length of the slot. If too wide, the blade tip may mar the work around the screw head. If too narrow or not thick enough, the screw slot and the tip of the blade will become burred. A blade that fits well may be kept in while turning the slot easier than one which does not.

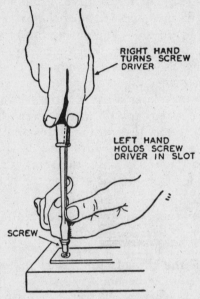

RIGHT HAND
TURNS SCREW
DRIVER

LEFT HAND
HOLDS SCREW
DRIVER IN SLOT

SCREW

Use Both Hands to Drive a Screw

More power can be applied with less effort with a long screw driver than with a short one. There is less danger that it will slip out of the slot. Of course limited space sometimes makes it impossible to use a long screw driver. Very short screw drivers called *stubbies* or *babies* are made for use in cramped spaces.

While it is true that a ten-cent screw driver is better than none at all, it really pays to buy a better one. The handle, the steel in the blade and the method of construction in a quality screw driver are much superior to the equivalent parts in a cheap tool. The blade of better steel will not become twisted or burred as easily. Moreover the tip of a good screw driver is ground so that the sides are practically parallel. A blade which tapers out from the tip too quickly has a tendency to raise out of the slot. It costs more to grind the sides of the blade parallel than it does to produce a blade with taper. A correctly ground blade is found only on the more expensive screw drivers.

Driving Screws. Use the *longest* screw driver available which is convenient for the work and whose blade *fits* the screw slot. Center the tip of the blade in the screw slot. Hold the handle of the screw driver firmly in the right hand with the head of the handle against the palm and the thumb and fingers grasping the handle near the ferrule. To drive a screw *in,* turn it *clockwise* which means in the same direction that the hands of the clock move. To remove or withdraw a screw, turn it in the opposite or counter-clockwise direction. When taking a fresh grip on the handle with the right hand, steady the tip of the screw driver and keep it pressed in the screw slot with the left hand. The left hand fingers should grasp the blade of the screw driver just above the tip. Relax their grip when the screw driver is turned. Tighten it while renewing the grip on the handle for a new turn.

A little soap rubbed into the threads of a wood screw makes it easier to drive. A drop of oil or a little graphite will do the same thing for a machine screw. Graphite and oil smeared in the threads of a steel machine screw will often prevent it from becoming rusted in and will make it easier to remove when necessary.

To Remove a Tight Screw. When a tight screw is to be removed and it cannot be turned at the first attempt, often it can be started if it is first given a *slight* twist in a clockwise direction, that is, in the direction which will drive it in. It is sometimes helpful if the screw is worked both ways. In other words, it should be backed out as far as it will go easily and then turned part way back in. It will usually back out a little farther each time this operation is repeated, until it is all the way out.

When a tight screw is to be withdrawn, a screw driver with a blade that has parallel sides and which fits the screw slot perfectly, *must* be used. Otherwise the slot of the screw will be "chewed" so that the job is doubly difficult. If a stubborn screw with a damaged slot can be backed out part way, it is sometimes possible to turn it the rest of the way with a pair of pliers.

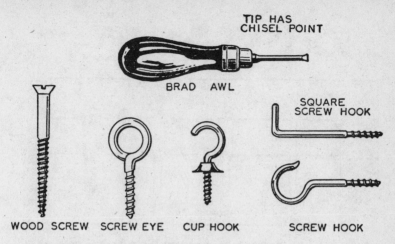

TIP HAS
CHISEL POINT

BRAD AWL

SQUARE
SCREW HOOK

WOOD SCREW   SCREW EYE   CUP HOOK   SCREW HOOK

Brad Awl

A brad awl is used to bore pilot holes in soft wood for small screws, screw eyes, screw hooks, cup hooks, etc.

Pilot Holes for Screws. If a wood screw is driven in without first boring a pilot hole for the threaded part, the wood may split and in some instances the screw head may be twisted off. Holes for small screws can be made with a small brad awl. Bore the holes for large screws with the bits or twist drills as in table on page 36. If the wood is soft (pine, spruce, basswood, tulip, etc.) bore the hole only about half as deep as the threaded part of the screw, as shown in the illustration on page 35. If the wood is hard (oak, maple, birch, etc.) the hole must be almost as deep as the screw.

In hard wood, if the screw is large or is a brass screw, it is necessary to bore a pilot hole slightly smaller in diameter than the threaded part of the screw and then enlarge the hole at the top with a second drill of the same diameter as the unthreaded portion of the screw. Instructions for using small drills are given in another chapter.

Fastening Wood with Screws. When two pieces of wood are to be fastened tightly together with screws, two sets of holes must be drilled. The holes are drilled so that the threaded portion of the screw "bites" or "takes hold" only in the under piece of wood. The piece on top is clamped to the lower piece only by the pressure of the screw head. This is illustrated in the drawing on this page. There are five steps in the operation.

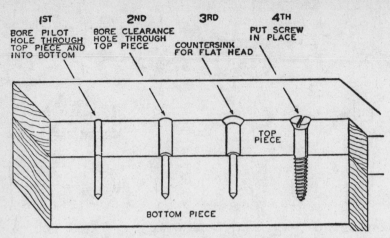

1ST
BORE PILOT HOLE THROUGH TOP PIECE AND INTO BOTTOM

2ND
BORE CLEARANCE HOLE THROUGH TOP PIECE

3RD
COUNTERSINK FOR FLAT HEAD

4TH
PUT SCREW IN PLACE

TOP PIECE

BOTTOM PIECE

THE STEPS IN FASTENING TWO PIECES OF
WOOD TOGETHER WITH SCREWS

1. Locate the position of the screw holes and mark them with a brad awl. The awl mark will center the drill and prevent it from "walking" away from the spot.

2. Bore a pilot hole, slightly smaller in diameter than the threaded portion of the screw, all the way through the upper piece of wood and into the lower piece half the length of the threaded part of the screw.

3. Enlarge the pilot hole in the upper piece of wood by drilling it out to the same diameter (or slightly larger) than the shank or unthreaded portion of the screw.

4. If flat head or oval head screws are to be used, countersink the clearance hole in the upper piece of wood to match the diameter of the heads of the screws. If round head screws or cup washers are used, do not countersink.

5. Drive all screws firmly in place and, after they are all in, tighten each of them.

To Fasten Hardware in Place. Certain hinges, striking plates, etc., require that the wood underneath be recessed before they can be mounted. Locate the position of the hardware on the work and score a line around it with the point of a sharp pen knife blade. Using this line as a guide, cut the recess with a chisel. The use of a chisel is explained in Chapter 6. Locate the position of the screws, mark with a brad awl and drill holes of the proper size for the screws. Drive the screws in place tightly.

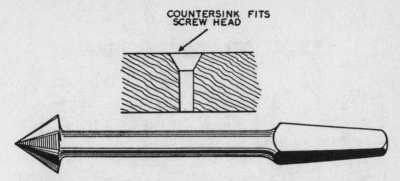

COUNTERSINK FOR FLAT HEAD AND OVAL HEAD SCREWS

The upper end of the pilot hole is bored out with a countersink to make room for the head of the screw. The countersink used for wood screws fits into a brace.

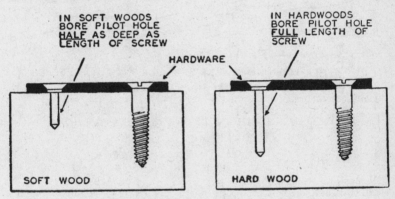

How to Fasten Hardware in Place

The wood is shown in section so that the pilot holes and screws are revealed.

When the work does not need to be recessed to fit the hardware piece, the proper procedure is:

1. Lay the hardware on the work in the correct position and mark the screw holes.

2. Bore pilot holes which are slightly smaller in diameter than the threaded portion of the screws. If the wood is soft, bore the pilot hole only as deep as half the length of the threaded part of the screw. If the wood is hard, bore the hole nearly as deep as the length of the screw. If the screws are short only a pilot hole will be needed, but long screws require a clearance hole of the same diameter and

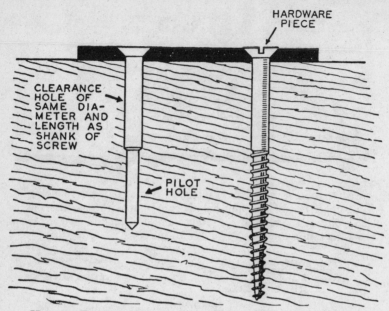

How to Fasten Hardware in Place with Long Screws

When long screws are used both pilot holes and clearance holes should be drilled.

Table Showing Sizes of Holes to Bore for Wood Screws

	Size of Screw				
	No. 4	No. 5	No. 6	No. 7	No. 8
Diameter of Gimlet, Auger or Twist Bit to use for Clearance Hole.	1/8″	1/8″	5/32″	5/32″	3/16″
Size Twist Drill to use for Clearance Hole.	No. 34	No. 30	No. 28	No. 24	No. 19
Diameter of Gimlet, Auger or Twist Bit to use for Pilot Hole.	1/16″	3/32″	3/32″	1/8″	1/8″

	Size of Screw			
	No. 9	No. 10	No. 11	No. 12
Diameter of Gimlet, Auger or Twist Bit to use for Clearance Hole.	3/16″	3/16″	7/32″	7/32″
Size Twist Drill to use for Clearance Hole.	No. 16	No. 11	No. 6	No. 2
Diameter of Gimlet, Auger or Twist Bit to use for Pilot Hole.	1/8″	1/8″	5/32″	5/32″

length as the shank or unthreaded part of the screw.

3. The size of the screws should be the largest size that will slip easily through the holes in the hardware unless the holes are countersunk. If countersunk, oval head or flat head screws to fit the countersink should be used. If the holes in the hardware are not countersunk, round head screws should be used.

4. Drive all the screws in but do not tighten them completely until all are in place.

Twisting Off of Brass Screws. Since a brass screw is not as strong as a steel screw, the head and shank will twist off more easily. This is apt to occur when a brass screw is driven into hardwood. Rubbing the threads on a cake of soap before the screw is put in place will help avoid this. A more certain method is to drive in a steel screw of the same size first. The steel screw is then removed and the brass screw put in its place. The steel screw cuts a thread in the wood into which the brass screw will go easily.

How to Conceal Screws. Screws are sometimes set below the surface of the wood and concealed by a wooden plug. The planking on a boat is usually fastened to the boat frames in this manner. Wooden plugs of various diameters, cut from mahogany, oak, pine, white cedar and cypress, can be purchased from dealers in boat supplies and at some hard-

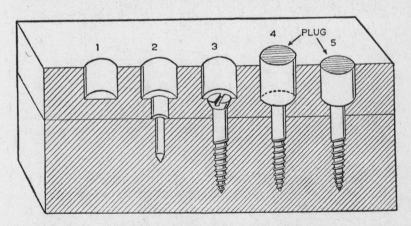

HOW TO CONCEAL SCREWS WITH WOODEN PLUGS
1. Bore hole to fit plug. 2. Bore pilot and clearance holes for screws. 3. Drive screw in place. 4. Drive plug in. Use glue. 5. When glue has dried, pare top of plug off even with surface.

ware stores. They can be cut with a tool called a plug cutter.
This tool fits into an ordinary brace. Plugs should be cut
from the same kind of wood as that in which they are to be
inserted and the grain should match as closely as possible.
They should be cut so that the grain runs across the plug
and not lengthwise.

First bore a hole at least 3/8″ deep with an auger bit of
the same size as the wooden plug. Then bore the proper
pilot and clearance holes for the screw. Put the screw in
place and drive it in as far as it will go with a screw driver.
Select a suitable plug, put some glue on its sides and insert
it into the hole with the grain on the end of the plug running
in the same direction as the grain on the surface of the
work. Drive the plug in as far as it will go. When the glue
has dried, use a chisel or a plane to pare the plug off level
with the surface.

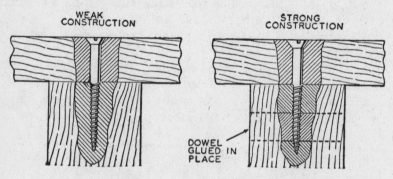

How to Make a Screw Hold in End Wood

A screw does not hold well in end wood. When the type of butt
joint shown in the left hand sketch must be fastened with a screw, it
can be greatly strengthened by the construction shown in the right
hand sketch. A hole is bored across grain and into this is driven a
tightly fitting dowel. The dowel is glued in place and located so that
the screw passes through it.

Misusing Screw Drivers. Until this point in our discussion we have talked about the common form of screw driver.
This has a long, slim, steel shank with a wood or plastic
handle and is used to loosen or tighten ordinary wood screws
and small machine screws. The handle is usually fastened
to the shank by a steel pin through the ferrule (the metal
band around the handle where the shank enters).

The ordinary screw driver will withstand considerable twisting strain but it is not intended for prying or chiselling. If used for prying, it will bend and it is usually difficult to make it perfectly straight again. A screw driver which is even slightly bent is difficult to keep in the slot of a screw.

When a screw driver is used as a substitute for a chisel or a punch and you hammer the handle, there is a good chance that the handle will split. If you must pry with an ordinary screw driver or hammer on the handle, use judgment so as not to strain it or, better still, keep an old screw driver on hand just for such purposes.

The tip of a screw driver blade is hardened to prevent it from becoming worn and burred. The tip is harder and more brittle than the rest of the shank. It will break if strained too much.

On the other hand, there is a rugged screw driver which will withstand a great deal of hard use and considerable abuse. It is used by automotive mechanics, machine repair men and assemblers. The shank goes all the way through the handle so that you can tap on it, if the occasion requires, without splitting the handle. When a rusty screw must be removed and the slot is full of rust, the tip of the blade may have to be seated in the slot by hitting the handle with a hammer. This is permissible if the steel shank extends through the handle.

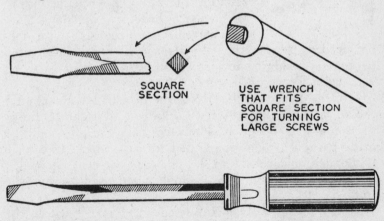

SQUARE
SECTION

USE WRENCH
THAT FITS
SQUARE SECTION
FOR TURNING
LARGE SCREWS

SQUARE SHANK SCREW DRIVER FOR LARGE SCREWS
Used by machinists and equally useful to a woodworker for driving large wood screws.

Some heavy duty machinists' screw drivers have a handle with a double grip so that both hands can be used to apply the force necessary to tighten or loosen an obstinate screw. There are also heavy duty screw drivers having a square shank which is extra large and strong so as to stand up under hard use. The shank is square so that you can use a wrench on it and apply enough turning force to loosen a large rusted screw.

Phillips Screws and Screw Drivers. Phillips screws have two slots which cross at the center. They are used to considerable extent in radio sets and on the moldings and trim of automobiles. Their advantage is that the screw driver cannot slip out of the slot and damage the finish. Phillips head screws require a Phillips screw driver. The tip of the blade is shaped like a cross and fits into both slots. It is necessary to use more downward pressure to keep a Phillips screw driver in the crossed slots than to keep the blade of an ordinary screw driver in the slot of an ordinary screw.

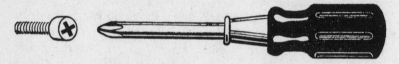

PHILLIPS SCREW AND SCREW DRIVER

Dressing a Screw Driver Blade Dressing is a term which mechanics use to mean putting in order or adjusting. Since a screw driver is not a cutting tool, it does not need to be resharpened. It must, however, be dressed or kept in condition by occasionally grinding or by filing with a flat file.

If filed, the screw driver must be held in a vise. The tip should be made straight across the end, at right angles to the shank and the sides. The faces near the tip should be made parallel or almost parallel to each other. If the tip is rounded or beveled and the sides are not nearly parallel, the screw driver will slip or climb out of and damage the slot.

When a screw driver is dressed on an emery wheel, the novice should remember not to hold the blade against the wheel too long. The friction may heat the steel and draw the temper so that the blade becomes soft. When the blade

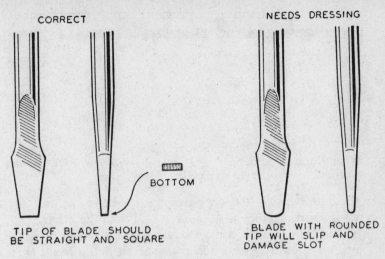

CORRECT   NEEDS DRESSING

BOTTOM

TIP OF BLADE SHOULD   BLADE WITH ROUNDED
BE STRAIGHT AND SQUARE   TIP WILL SLIP AND
                                 DAMAGE SLOT

A Screw Driver Blade with Rounded
Tip Needs Dressing

is being ground, dip it in water frequently to cool it. If the blade becomes so hot that it discolors (blue or yellow) the temper has been damaged.

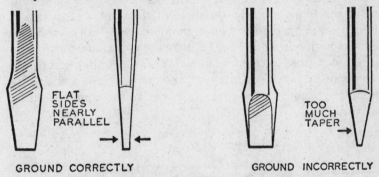

FLAT
SIDES
NEARLY
PARALLEL

TOO
MUCH
TAPER

GROUND CORRECTLY   GROUND INCORRECTLY

How to Dress a Screw Driver Blade

File or grind the blade so that the flat sides are parallel or taper very slightly back of the tip.

Offset Screw Drivers. Hidden screws or screws located where there is not sufficient space to use an ordinary screw driver can often be manipulated with an offset screw driver. This tool is usually made from a piece of round or octagonal steel with two blades at right angles to one another at opposite ends. In a very cramped place it may be necessary

OFFSET SCREW DRIVER

When space is too cramped to use an ordinary screw driver, screws can often be manipulated with an offset screw driver.

to use both ends of the screw driver, alternately turning the screw a short distance with one end and then the other.

Screw Driver Bits. Large screws can be driven or withdrawn more easily with a screw driver bit and a brace than with a screw driver. The brace provides more leverage than a screw driver. A screw driver bit is a screw driver blade with a square shank at one end so that it will fit in the chuck on a brace. Bits are made in several widths from 3/16" to 3/4" to fit screws from No. 4 to No. 26 and larger. The bit should fit the slot of the screw snugly and should be of the same width as the head of the screw. It is important for the bit blade to be in good shape. A twisted blade or one with a rounded or beveled tip will climb out of the screw slot and damage the screw so that it cannot be turned. A screw driver bit is dressed and kept in good shape by filing or grinding in the same manner as the common screw driver.

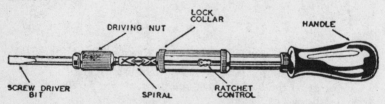

AUTOMATIC SCREW DRIVER

Pushing the handle turns the blade. It can be used both to drive and withdraw screws. The mechanism can be locked so that the tool can be used as an ordinary screw driver.

Wood Screws and Machine Screws

Screws may be divided into two general groups; those designed for fastening wood and those made for metal. The former

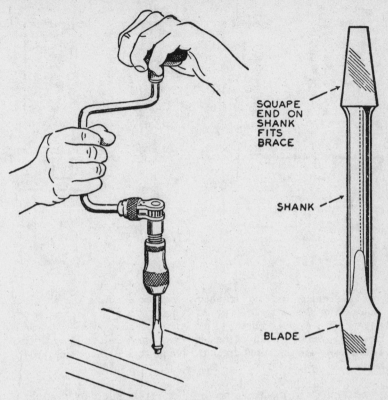

SQUARE
END ON
SHANK
FITS
BRACE

SHANK

BLADE

SCREW DRIVER BIT FOR BRACE

The brace provides greater leverage than an ordinary screw driver and requires less effort to drive.

are called wood screws, the latter machine screws. A wood screw cuts its own thread into the material into which it is screwed. A machine screw does not cut its own thread. It must be provided with a threaded hole. Both hole and thread must fit the screw. A machine screw has no holding power unless a hole is first drilled and threaded for it.

Wood Screws. The two most common wood screws are the flat head and round head, so-called because of the shape of their heads. Wood screws are sized according to diameter and length. The length is indicated in inches or fractions thereof. The diameter is indicated by a number. The smallest diameter is No. 0 and the largest common size is No. 24. The most generally used sizes are Nos. 3 to 16.

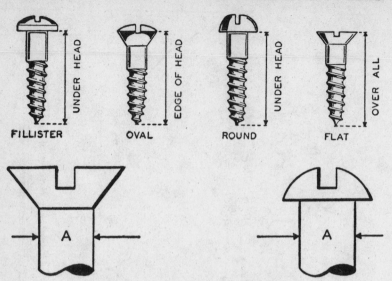

FILLISTER   OVAL   ROUND   FLAT

How to Measure a Wood Screw

The diameter or gage number is measured across the shank as indicated in the illustration by A. The length of a flat head wood screw is the overall length. The length of an oval head screw is measured from the point to the edge of the head. Round and fillister head screws are measured from the points to the under sides of the heads.

Standards for screws have been established by co-operation between the manufacturers and the U. S. Bureau of Standards so that standard screws of all screw manufacturers are alike.

The following table shows the diameter of wood screws indicated by the numbers 0 to 24. The dimension in the left-hand column is the basic dimension. A certain amount of tolerance or variation in size is allowed in manufacturing. The second and third columns show the maximum and minimum diameter a screw of each size can have within the limits of the standard.

The diameter of a wood screw is measured across the shank as indicated in the illustration by A.

In addition to flat head and round head wood screws there are also oval head and fillister head screws. The length of a flat head wood screw is the over-all length, but the length of round and fillister head screws is measured from the point to the under side of the head. The length of an oval head screw is measured from the point to the edge of the head.

THE DIAMETER OF STANDARD WOOD SCREWS

Number	Basic	Maximum	Minimum
		Diameter	
0	.060	.064	.053
1	.073	.077	.066
2	.086	.090	.079
3	.099	.103	.092
4	.112	.116	.105
5	.125	.129	.118
6	.138	.142	.131
7	.151	.155	.144
8	.164	.168	.157
9	.177	.181	.170
10	.190	.194	.183
11	.203	.207	.196
12	.216	.220	.209
14	.242	.246	.235
16	.268	.272	.261
18	.294	.298	.287
20	.320	.324	.313
24	.372	.376	.365

14 12 10 9 8 7 6 5 4 3 2 1

WOOD SCREWS

These full-size sketches may be used to identify Nos. 1 to 14 wood screws.

Lag Screws and Hanger Bolts. Lag screws have square heads like machine bolts and are driven in place or withdrawn with a wrench instead of a screw driver. They are used in heavy construction where great strength is required. They are also used to fasten machinery and heavy metal parts to beams, walls and wooden floors. A pilot hole should be drilled for a lag screw. When two pieces of timber are to be held together by lag screws, both a pilot hole and a clearance hole should be drilled as though ordinary wood screws were being used. A metal washer should be placed under the head of a lag screw so that the head will not cut its way into the wood when it is tightened.

Lag screws are sized according to diameter and length. The common diameters are 1/4", 5/16", 3/8", 7/16",

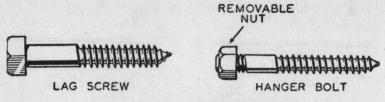

LAG SCREW   HANGER BOLT

Screws for Heavy Construction Which Are Driven with a Wrench

1/2″ and 5/8″. Common lengths range from 2″ to 6″ in half-inch steps and from 6″ to 12″ in one-inch steps. Lag screws are made in black iron, galvanized iron, forged bronze and Everdur bronze.

The head of a hanger bolt is a hexagonal nut which can readily be removed with a wrench. Hanger bolts are used for fastening machinery and other heavy metal pieces to a wooden foundation. If a lag screw is driven in and out of the same hole several times, it loses some of its holding

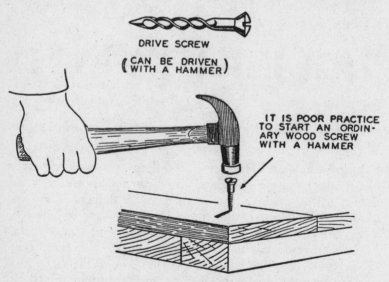

DRIVE SCREW

(CAN BE DRIVEN)
(WITH A HAMMER)

IT IS POOR PRACTICE TO START AN ORDINARY WOOD SCREW WITH A HAMMER

Driving Screws with a Hammer

Small screws may be started in soft wood without boring a pilot hole by driving them part way in with a hammer. This is practical where it is not necessary to secure the maximum holding power of a screw but generally it is bad practice and should be avoided. A drive screw, illustrated above, is a special screw which can be driven into wood like a nail.

power. In order to remove a machine fastened with hanger bolts, it is unnecessary to withdraw the whole bolt. Only the nut which forms the head is unscrewed. Thus a machine secured with hanger bolts may be removed and replaced innumerable times without the bolt losing any of its holding power.

---

3   How to Use a Hand Saw

PRACTICALLY everyone is familiar with the standard hand saw. Some men and boys will consider it as presumptuous to tell them how to saw as it would be to tell them how to walk or run. But whereas walking may consist of moving your legs back and forth, sawing is not merely pushing a saw to and fro. You can cut good firewood that way, but to cut woodwork accurately you have to use your eye and your head as well as your muscles. Accurate sawing requires a knack which is acquired by knowledge and practice. When you have the knack it is easy to cut a piece off a 10- or 12-inch plank to accurate length and find upon checking it with a try square that the end is at 90 degrees with the top, bottom and sides. Many carpenters, who can cut a piece of work perfectly square or at an accurate angle for a mitre joint as at the corner of a picture frame, would find it difficult to cut some of the double angles which a skillful boat builder does with apparent ease.

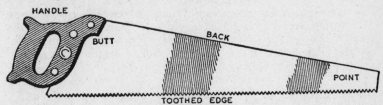

HAND SAWS

The blade of a good hand saw is not a flat piece of steel of even thickness. It tapers from the tooth edge to the back and from the butt to the point along the back. The tooth edge is the same thickness along its entire length.

The Right Saw for the Job. The wooden portion you grip in your hand when sawing is the handle. The toothed steel portion which extends from the handle and does the cutting is the blade.

To the skilled mechanic there is only one saw intended for each specific job. The stair builder and the boat builder use special saws in their work which neither the carpenter nor ordinary woodworker needs. The correct tool always makes work easier. It saves time and energy and produces better results.

The grain of wood must be taken into consideration in all woodworking operations. All wood has grain. The same saw will not cut equally well across the grain and with the grain. Therefore there are two types of hand saws for wood. One, called a *rip* saw, is made to saw in the direction of the grain which usually runs lengthwise in a piece of wood. The other, called a *cross-cut* saw is used for cutting across grain.

CROSSCUT

RIP

CROSS-CUT AND RIP SAWS

By examining the teeth you can distinguish between a cross-cut saw (for cutting across grain) and a rip saw (for cutting with the grain). The teeth of a cross-cut saw are sharpened at a bevel so that they are pointed like the end of a knife blade. The teeth of a rip saw are sharpened like chisels.

You can distinguish between a rip saw and a cross-cut saw by examining the teeth. A rip saw usually has larger teeth than a cross-cut saw of the same length. In both types the teeth are set alternately to the left and right so as to cut a kerf (the slot which the saw forms) which is wider than the thickness of the blade. The teeth on a rip saw are given

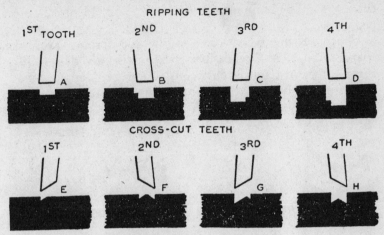

RIPPING TEETH

1ST TOOTH 2ND 3RD 4TH

A B C D

CROSS-CUT TEETH

1ST 2ND 3RD 4TH

E F G H

How Saw Teeth Cut

The teeth of a cross-cut saw first cut across the fibers, then remove the wood. If the first tooth which strikes the wood is set to the left, the point will cut across the fibers and make an incision as at E in the illustration. The following tooth will cut across the fibers to the right as at F. The teeth which follow deepen the incisions and chisel out the wood as shown by G and H.

When a cut is made with a rip saw, if the first tooth striking the wood is set to the left, it will make a groove as shown at A. The next tooth will enlarge the groove as shown at B. The following teeth will make the groove deeper as shown at C and D.

less set than the teeth on a cross-cut saw. If you look closely at them you will see that they are shaped like chisels. In fact, they cut exactly like a gang of small vertical chisels arranged in a row.

The teeth of a cross-cut saw are sharpened at a bevel so that they are pointed like the end of a knife blade. This provides two lines of sharp points which cut across the wood fibers like knives. The teeth then force out the wood between the two cuts.

There are four common sizes of hand saws. The size is the length of the tooth edge measured in inches. The popular sizes are 24″ and 26″.

The coarseness or fineness of a saw depends upon the size of the teeth and is designated by the number of tooth points per inch. The saw having few teeth—5, 5 1/2, 6 or 7 points to the inch—will cut fast but make a rough cut. Rip saws usually are in this category. The common hand cross-cut saw can be obtained with either 8, 9, 10, 11 or 12 points per inch.

Green or wet wood can best be cut across grain with coarse teeth (6 or 7 points per inch) having a wide set. Dry, seasoned wood requires fine teeth (10 or 11 points per inch) having a narrow set. A fine-tooth saw is better for smooth accurate cutting.

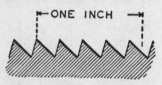 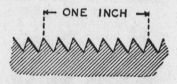

5½-POINT RIP TEETH   8-POINT CROSS CUT TEETH

THE SIZE OF THE SAW TEETH

The term "points to the inch" indicates the size of the teeth. For ordinary cross-cut work a 6- or 8-point saw is used but for finer work 10 or 12 points are better. A rip saw having 5½ points to the inch will cut rapidly and easily in pine and other soft woods. For ripping oak, cherry, mahogany and other hard woods, a 6- or 7-point saw is most satisfactory.

For general work, a 24″ or 26″ rip saw with 5 1/2 or 6 points to the inch, and a 24″ or 26″ cross-cut saw with 8 or 9 points to the inch, are most widely used.

Quality saws are taper ground so that the steel blade is thinner at the back than at the toothed edge. A tapered blade makes a saw easier to push back and forth in the kerf.

The Care of Saws. Moisture on the blade of a saw, unless the surface is well protected by a film of oil, produces rust almost immediately. Rust will pit and roughen the smooth sides of a saw blade. Both sides must be smooth in order for a saw to be in perfect working condition. At the first appearance of any rust spots on a saw blade, rub them off with fine emery cloth and apply a coat of light oil. Keep your saws in a dry place and hang them up when not in use. Especially in the summer, an unoiled saw blade will rust if it is not used constantly. When you lay a saw down, do so carefully. Do not drop it.

A dull saw makes hard work of sawing. A saw cuts with ease when properly sharpened and set. Keep it that way. Instructions for sharpening and setting are in Chapter 10.

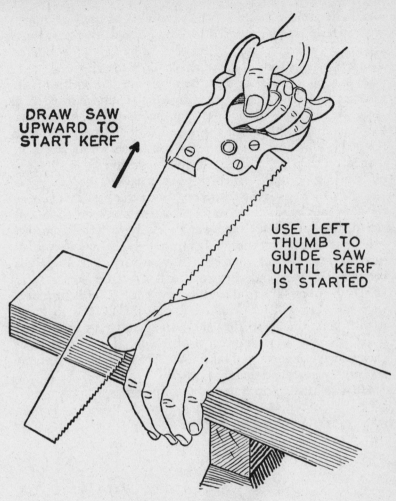

DRAW SAW
UPWARD TO
START KERF

USE LEFT
THUMB TO
GUIDE SAW
UNTIL KERF
IS STARTED

STARTING THE KERF

Sawing Before a piece of wood can be sawed to accurate size or shape, it must be marked with a line which will serve as a guide for the saw cut. Rough work can be marked with a pencil. Use a try square as a guide for the pencil if the cut is to be made at right angles and a sliding T-bevel if the cut is to be made at an angle other than 90 degrees.

A pencil line is easy to see, but when drawn on wood it is too thick for close work. For accurate work or small work, the mark should be scored into the wood with a scratch awl. The point of a knife blade can also be used. A marking gauge is frequently used in laying out work for sawing, especially when making a mortise, a tenon or a rabbet. The use of this tool is explained in Chapter 7.

In sawing, allowance must be made for the width of the saw cut or kerf. Do not saw directly on the marked line. Accurate sawing is always done on the waste side of the line. Sawing on the line or on the wrong side of the line makes the stock too short. If you leave too much wood, it can be planed or chiseled off. But if you leave too little, there is no "putting on tool" which will put it back.

How to Use a Cross-Cut Saw. Start the kerf by drawing the saw backward across an edge of the stock on the waste side of the line. Guide the blade carefully with the tip or the first joint of the left thumb, bearing in mind that if you are careless you may cut yourself. In cross-cutting, a 45° angle between the saw and the work will give the best results. It may be necessary to draw the saw back several times before the kerf will be properly started. Continue to guide it with your thumb so that the kerf is started at the exact point where you wish the cut to begin. Draw the blade back slowly. A too rapid motion may cause the saw to jump and give you a sore thumb.

How to Use a Rip Saw. If the rip saw is a coarse one it

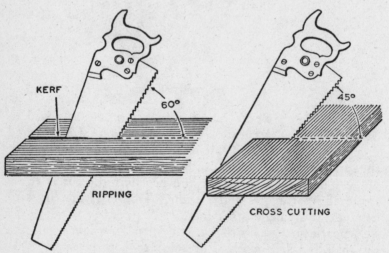

THE CORRECT SAWING ANGLES

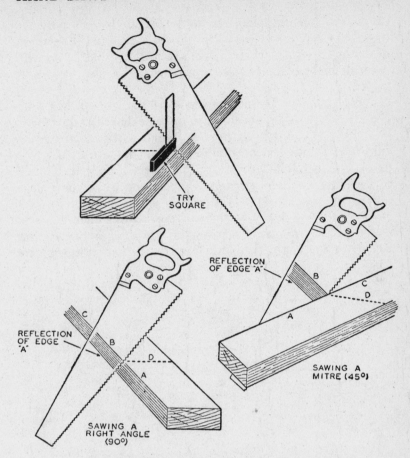

HINTS FOR SAWING STRAIGHT

Keep checking the position of the saw with a try square from time to time until tests show you can saw straight without its aid. Reflections in a polished saw blade can be used to ascertain its correct position. When sawing at a right angle (along the line D in lower left hand sketch) the image (B) of the edge of the wood reflected on the side of the blade will appear continuous with the real edge AC. When sawing at 45 degrees (along the line D in the right hand sketch) the image (B) of the edge of the wood reflected on the blade will be perpendicular to the edge AC.

will have a few fine teeth at the end farthest from the handle, which end, incidentally, is usually referred to as the point of the saw. The cut should be started with the fine teeth at the point of the saw by drawing them back several times in the manner already described for starting the cross-cut saw. When ripping, an angle of 60 degrees between the blade and the work gives the best results. The teeth of either the cross-cut or the rip saw will cut most efficiently only when the blade is held approximately at the angle suggested.

Hints for Sawing   The piece to be sawed must be held firmly in a vise, or on a workbench, a box or a pair of horses. Small work often can be held firmly on a bench or table by the pressure of the left hand. A bench hook for this purpose (see sketch) is a great convenience. Pieces of considerable length are best supported on a pair of saw horses, or on two boxes or two chairs, and held firmly by the pressure of one knee.

As a saw progresses across the grain of a board, the weight of the board tends to close the cut and bind the saw

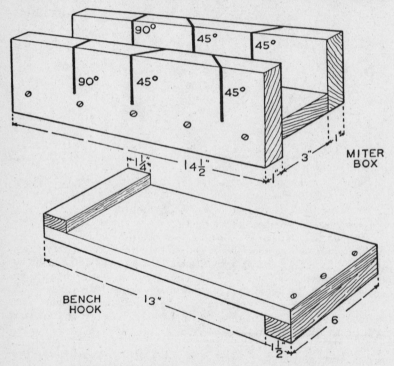

HOMEMADE BENCH HOOK AND MITRE BOX

These useful aids to sawing should preferably be made of hard wood. Although both sketches are dimensioned, they can be made any convenient size. The front of the mitre box projects below the bottom so that it can be hooked against the edge of the workbench.

so that you can no longer push the blade back and forth. If the waste end is a short, light piece you can hold it up with your left hand while sawing and prevent the slot from closing on the blade. You will need an assistant to hold a long or heavy piece. Moreover, if you do not support the waste end properly, it will break off just as you are finishing the cut and take a large splinter from the corner of the other piece with it. The splinter can be glued back in place but it is preferable to avoid this.

The proper position for sawing permits long easy strokes using nearly the full length of the blade. Take your time, and be careful not to jerk the saw back and forth. It is difficult to keep the kerf beside the marked line where it belongs if much of the cutting is done with only a few inches of the blade.

Watch your grip on the handle closely when you are learning to saw. It should be firm but not tight. The saw should run freely. A tight grip prevents the free running of the saw and tends to swerve the blade away from the line. The thumb should be against the left side of the handle. Keep the index finger extended along the right side of the handle to help guide the blade. If the blade starts to cut into the marked line or to move too far away from it, twist the handle slightly in order to draw it back to the correct position.

To keep the saw at right angles to the surface of the work is the most difficult thing to learn in sawing. The beginner should make an occasional test with a try square, as shown in one of the illustrations, to keep the saw in a perfectly vertical position and to help develop the knack of sawing square. Check the position of the blade with the try square from time to time until the tests show that you can get along without it. That stage in your skill will not be reached the first few times that you use a saw. It will come only with careful practice. Accurate sawing is done with long, easy, relaxed strokes, guided by the hand and eye, and is mastered only with practice.

All the cutting action of the teeth on a hand saw takes place on the forward or pushing stroke of the saw blade. Do not try to make the teeth cut on the backward or pulling stroke. Exert a little downward pressure of the wrist on the forward stroke and do not apply any pressure on the return stroke. Do not try to guide the blade on the return stroke. Relax and lift it more than pull it. If the tip of the blade vibrates when the blade is brought back on the return stroke, you are not allowing the saw to run freely but are bending or twisting it slightly.

Look carefully for nails in the path of the saw when second hand lumber is used or repair work is done. A hand saw will not cut nails. If it is drawn or pushed over a nail, the sharp points and edges will be knocked off the teeth.

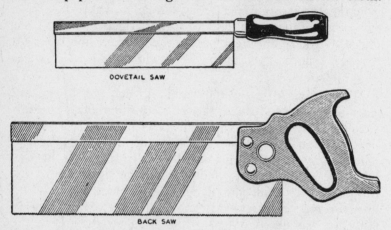

DOVETAIL SAW

BACK SAW

SAWS FOR FINE ACCURATE WORK

Back Saws for Fine Accurate Work   A back saw is a thin-bladed cross-cut saw with fine teeth, stiffened by a thick steel rib on the back edge. A dovetail saw is a small edition of a back saw. Both tools are used for cutting light stock, moldings and picture frames and for dovetailing, tenoning, pattern making, fine joinery, cabinet work and model making.

Back saws range in size from a blade length of 8″ with 16 points to the inch to a blade of 16″ with 12 points to the inch. A popular size for fairly smooth accurate cutting of light stock, making mitres, tenons, etc., is the 12″ with 14 points per inch.

Dovetail Saws. Dovetail saws range in length from 6″ to 12″ and have 17 points per inch.

Mitre Box Saws. Mitre box saws are long back saws (20″ to 28″) made for use with a mitre box.

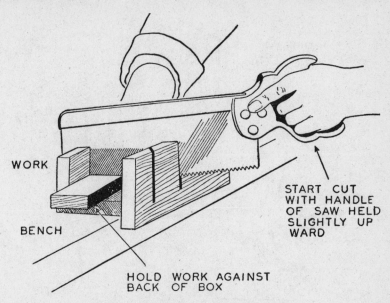

WORK

BENCH

START CUT
WITH HANDLE
OF SAW HELD
SLIGHTLY UP
WARD

HOLD WORK AGAINST
BACK OF BOX

Using a Back Saw and Mitre Box

The simplest form of mitre box is made of three pieces of wood fastened together so as to form a trough, open at the top and both ends. It has several vertical saw slots in the sides which act as guides for the saw blade and hold it at the proper angle to make either a square or 45-degree cut. A 12″ or 14″ back saw can be used with the average, small homemade mitre box. The long mitre box saws are made for use with the more elaborate adjustable factory-made mitre boxes.

To saw off a piece of wood square or at an angle of 45 degrees in a wooden mitre box, put the work in the box in position so that the cut to be made lines up with the proper slots in the box. Hold the work firmly against the bottom and the back of the box as pictured in the drawing. Start the cut slowly and carefully, using the back stroke and holding the handle of the saw upward until the kerf is established. Then begin sawing, gradually lower the handle until the blade is horizontal and finish the cut with it in that position.

When a back saw is used without a mitre box, it is advisable to hold the work in a vise or use a bench hook to prevent it from slipping.

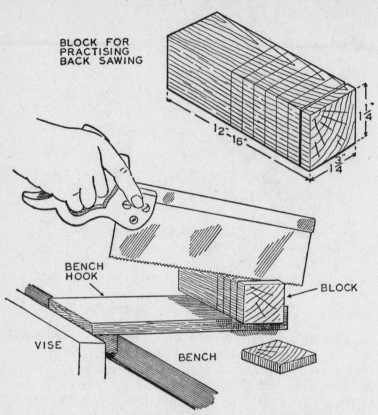

BLOCK FOR
PRACTISING
BACK SAWING

1 1/4"

12" 16"

3/4"

BENCH
HOOK

BLOCK

VISE

BENCH

PRACTICE TO ACQUIRE SKILL WITH A BACK SAW

Practice for Back Saw Skill Pattern makers and cabinet makers use back saws with great skill for light or fine work and for fitting and dovetailing. Their tool kits usually contain at least two back saws, one filed for crosscutting, and the other filed for ripsawing or cutting with the grain of the wood, as in the cutting of tenons and dovetails.

The woodworking beginner who will carefully practice with a back saw can learn to use this tool with skill in a few hours.

The guide line for sawing with a back saw is always scored with a knife. A pencil line is not fine enough for the accurate work which can be done with a back saw.

Good exercise for practicing with a back saw is to cut thin sections from the end of a block of wood. Take a block of white pine about 1 3/4" square and from 12" to 16" long. Lay it out as shown in the illustration by scoring lines with a try square and a sharp-pointed pocketknife on the front upper and back surfaces. The lines should be about 1/4" apart and cut at least 1/32" deep. These lines are the guide lines for cutting the sections. The thumb of the left hand is used as a guide for the saw in starting the saw cut on the far edge of the stock. In starting the saw cut the handle of the saw is raised slightly as shown in the illustration. As the cut progresses, the saw is lowered gradually to a horizontal position. The saw cut through the block should be true to each of the three lines and the kerf should be close to but just a hair outside the knife line. If the sawing is done accurately, the saw teeth should not scratch any of the knife cuts but at the same time should be so close that there is no wood left projecting beyond the knife cut which must be smoothed down with plane or chisel.

A simple trick which will aid in getting a back saw started so as to make a straight and accurate cut is to cut a triangular groove on the waste side of the scored line. The groove can be made with either a pocketknife or chisel.

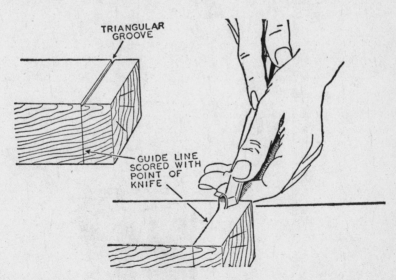

A HELP IN SECURING A STRAIGHT AND ACCURATE CUT
WITH A BACK SAW
Cut a triangular groove on the waste side of the scored line. Start the saw in the groove.

Compass and Keyhole Saws The narrow tapered blade of a compass saw is used for cutting curves or cutting holes started from a hole bored in the work. This tool comes with a fixed blade or with a removable blade which can be used in reverse position for undercutting. The teeth have considerable set so that they cut almost equally well with or across the grain. The blade length varies from 10″ to 16″. The teeth usually have 8 or 9 points to the inch.

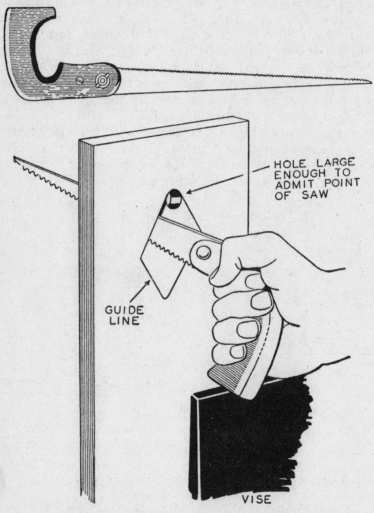

HOLE LARGE
ENOUGH TO
ADMIT POINT
OF SAW

GUIDE
LINE

VISE

A Compass Saw for Cutting Curves and Holes

Keyhole Saws. A keyhole saw is like a compass saw but smaller. Usually it has a straight handle. Its 10" or 12" removable blade with 10 teeth to the inch is made very narrow for small work in close quarters, such as cutting keyholes, sharp curves, fret work, etc.

When dismantling old woodwork for repairs or alterations, a compass saw or keyhole saw sometimes is used to start a kerf which is enlarged until a hand saw can be inserted. First, a hole is bored with an auger bit; then a compass or keyhole saw is inserted in the hole and the kerf started. When the cut is long enough, a regular hand saw is brought into use.

To cut a keyhole in a door or drawer, first mark the outline of the hole in the desired position. Bore a hole through the door or drawer large enough to pass the blade of the keyhole saw. Then cut along the marked line with the saw.

Coping Saws   A coping saw takes narrow blades 1/8" wide which are held in a frame similar to that of a hacksaw and which may be replaced quickly when dull. A coping saw is used to cut curves and intricate patterns in thin wood. Carpenters sometimes use this tool for shaping or "returning" the ends of molding.

It is customary to place the blades in the frame with the teeth pointing toward the handle so that they cut when the handle is pulled and not when it is pushed. This is the opposite of an ordinary saw and is the way Chinese and Japanese hand saws work. The arrangement gives better control of the small blade.

There are two types of coping saws. One has a frame made of heavy wire and takes blades having a loop at each end which fits into a slot in the frame. The blades are pulled out straight and held under tension by the spring of the frame. The other type of coping saw has a rigid frame and the blade is kept under tension by a threaded stretcher which is adjusted by turning the handle. The blade is fitted at its ends with pins which slip into slots in the stretcher at each end of the frame. If the blade is strained tight in the frame, it may be turned to prevent snapping when making sharp turns while sawing.

Blades for this frame are made either to cut wood only, or to cut wood, Bakelite, brass, bone, celluloid, copper, etc.

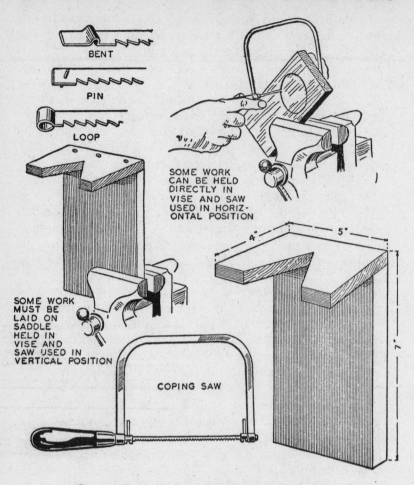

BENT

PIN

LOOP

SOME WORK
CAN BE HELD
DIRECTLY IN
VISE AND SAW
USED IN HORIZ-
ONTAL POSITION

SOME WORK
MUST BE
LAID ON
SADDLE
HELD IN
VISE AND
SAW USED IN
VERTICAL POSITION

COPING SAW

CoPING Saw; CoPING Saw Blades; Wooden
Saddle to Support Work

A coping saw is usually worked up and down so that the
blade moves vertically. The work is supported on a saddle
which is held in a vise or screwed to a workbench. A saddle
for this purpose is shown in an illustration. It consists of
two pieces of board fastened together so as to form an L.
The short board is cut with a V shaped notch about 3 or 4
inches wide and the same depth. The work to be sawed is
marked with the design to be followed by the saw and held
on the saddle so that the saw blade can work up and down
in the notch. Since the cutting is done on the down stroke,

the work is not lifted from the saddle by the motion of the blade. The work is turned and shifted from time to time to keep the saw blade in the V notch and to accommodate the curves as they are encountered.

4 How to Adjust and Use Planes

THERE is something fascinating about the sound of a plane and the manner in which the shavings curl out of it. The fresh, pleasant smell of wood rises to your nostrils. Almost everyone who has watched a carpenter using a plane has had an urge to get his own hands on the tool and make his own shavings.

However, the technique of planing involves more than making shavings. Know how is necessary. It is necessary to know how to adjust, how to hold and how to push one of these indispensable tools in order to produce good workmanship. In principle, a plane is a kind of chisel set in a block of wood or metal which acts as a guide to regulate the depth of the cut. A chisel-like plane "iron" does the cutting. This must have a keen edge and be correctly adjusted, and the whole tool must be controlled properly.

There are several types of planes. Each has a special purpose. The three most common are: the block plane, the smoothing plane and the jack plane. All are made on the same principle but differ in size and in use. The general purpose of a plane is to smooth off rough surfaces and bring woodwork to exact size after it has first been roughed out to approximate size. For example, it is not possible to make a close fit with a hand saw alone. A hand saw does not cut to accurate size and it leaves a rough, uneven surface. But the sawed edges can be smoothed with a plane and brought to close dimensions.

There are also planes for special purposes, such as the rabbet and cabinetmaker's planes used for cutting rabbets, tongues, grooves and moldings; low angle planes, circular planes, scrub planes, etc. All are described in this chapter.

Old-fashioned planes were made with wood frames. The modern plane has a cast iron frame which is preferable.

Holding the Work. While being planed, work should be so firmly secured that it cannot move. Accurate planing requires the use of both hands to guide the tool when the jack, smoothing, fore or jointer plane is used. A skilled woodworker can hold a short length of board on its edge with one hand and use the other to drive the plane but that ability comes only with experience. The novice will find that the most efficient way to hold work when planing is to clamp it in a bench vise.

The most desirable bench for woodworking is one provided with two quick-acting vises. One vise is attached to the front of the bench and the other to the right end. The vises may be of either wood or iron, the latter, equipped with an adjustable dog, being preferable. The vise dog is a square steel pin which can be moved up and down in a slot in the vise jaw. The dog can be set flush with the top of the jaw or raised above it. A row of holes into which a bench stop can be pushed should be cut in the top of the bench. The row should be in line with the dog on the end vise and parallel to the front edge of the bench. This arrangement permits boards to be clamped between the dog on the end vise and a bench stop located in one of the holes.

A hole for a bench stop near the left-hand front edge of the bench is also useful. It provides a firm rest against which a board can be held for planing when close accuracy is not needed.

A thin strip of wood nailed across the bench can also be used as a stop.

The Block Plane   This is the smallest and the simplest of the three common planes. It is held in one hand and in general it is used to plane small pieces of wood and end grain. Because the plane iron (the chisel-shaped cutter) is set at a lower angle than that of other planes, it will cut end grain better. It is the proper tool to use for making chamfers on small pieces of wood, for planing the ends of moldings and trim and for shaping the hulls and spars of model boats.

Before discussing the adjustment and handling of the block plane, let us examine one. It has a chisel-shaped plane

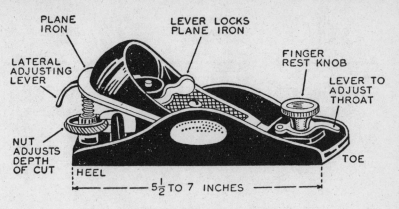

PLANE
IRON

LEVER LOCKS
PLANE IRON

FINGER
REST KNOB

LATERAL
ADJUSTING
LEVER

LEVER TO
ADJUST
THROAT

NUT
ADJUSTS
DEPTH
OF CUT

HEEL

TOE

5½ TO 7 INCHES

THE BLOCK PLANE IS THE SMALLEST
OF THE COMMON PLANES

It is used to smooth end grain, make chamfers and shape small
pieces of wood.

iron set at a low angle in an iron frame. Notice particularly
that the iron is a single blade. The plane iron in a jack plane
or a smoothing plane is double, for reasons which will be explained later. The blade in a block plane is locked in position by a lever cap or a lever cam. This detail will vary.
slightly in planes produced by different manufacturers.
Moving the lever cap screw or the lever, whichever the
plane may have, in one direction will lock the plane iron.
Moving the lever or screw in the opposite direction unlocks
the blade so that it can be removed from the frame. There
is a slot in the plane bottom which is known both as the
throat and as the mouth. The width of the throat is adjustable on some planes. The sharpened lower edge of the
plane iron can be moved in or out of the mouth by means
of an adjusting screw. Turning this screw controls the
thickness of the shavings. The shavings curl up through the
throat.

The sharpened edge of the plane iron is beveled on one
side only. It is set in the frame with the bevel *up*. In the
jack and smoothing planes, because the iron is at a greater
angle, it is set bevel *down*.

How to Adjust a Block Plane. Hold the plane bottom
side up in the left hand with the toe or front of the plane
toward you and the bottom level with the eye. Sight along
the bottom and with the right hand turn the adjusting screw

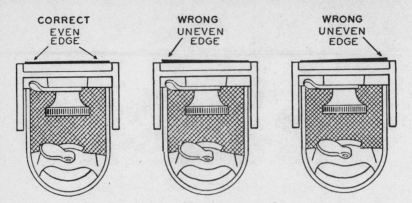

To Adjust the Thickness of Shavings

These are sketches of the bottom of a block plane. If the cutting edge projects unevenly it will make an uneven shaving. The cutting edges in the two right hand sketches are uneven and need adjusting with the lateral adjusting lever.

until the sharp edge of the blade or plane iron projects *slightly* through the throat and above the bottom of the plane. The most common mistake made by the novice in attempting to adjust a plane is setting the blade too far out. You should be able to see only its edge or to feel it just perceptibly by moving the fingertips very lightly across the bottom of the plane. If the blade is sharp, it will make thin shavings when properly set. Furthermore, much better results will be obtained if the plane is adjusted in this manner.

The blade's adjustment made to regulate the thickness of the shavings is called the vertical adjustment. The lateral adjustment is made to produce even shavings. It is meant to prevent one edge from being thicker than the other. To make a lateral adjustment, loosen the lever cap screw or the lever cam slightly and sight along the bottom of the plane. Press the upper end of the blade (near the adjusting screw) to the right or left, whichever is necessary to bring the cutting edge of the blade parallel with the bottom of the plane. Do not set one corner of the blade farther out of the throat than the other.

How to Hold a Block Plane. One hand only is used to guide and push a block plane. The sides of the plane are grasped between the thumb and the second and third fingers. The forefinger should rest in the hollow of the finger rest at the front of the plane. The finger rest is usually the hol-

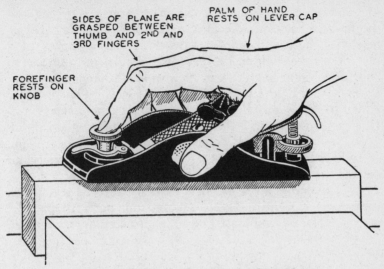

SIDES OF PLANE ARE
GRASPED BETWEEN
THUMB AND 2ND AND
3RD FINGERS

PALM OF HAND
RESTS ON LEVER CAP

FOREFINGER
RESTS ON
KNOB

A Block Plane Is Gripped in One Hand

lowed out top of the thumbscrew which locks the throat-adjusting lever. The lever cap should rest under the palm of the hand.

If your hand and eye are skillful enough to guide the plane firmly and accurately, you will have no trouble. You may, however, have to practice a great deal before you can plane properly. Press down and forward at the beginning

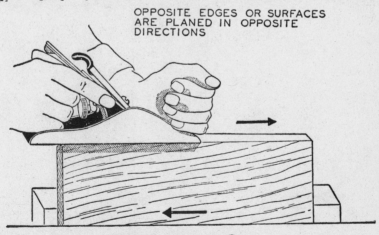

OPPOSITE EDGES OR SURFACES
ARE PLANED IN OPPOSITE
DIRECTIONS

PLANE WITH THE GRAIN

If the grain is torn or roughened by the plane, reverse the direction in which the plane is pushed.

of the stroke and *maintain the same pressure* throughout the forward motion. An even pressure is essential. Beginners are likely to bear down hard at the beginning of a planing stroke, lighten the pressure toward the center and bear down again at the end. Some do the opposite—bear down harder at the center than at the ends. The result of either of these mistakes will be a convex or concave surface instead of a straight one. Practice planing on pieces of scrap wood. Check your work with a try square and straight edge. Woodworking is easy enough if you first master the simple fundamentals.

As you know, all wood has a grain (direction in which the fibers run) and the grain seldom runs perfectly parallel with a surface. You must take this into consideration when

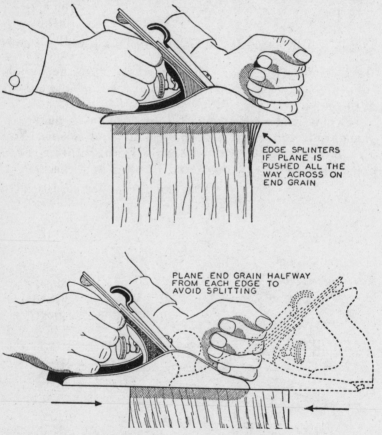

EDGE SPLINTERS
IF PLANE IS
PUSHED ALL THE
WAY ACROSS ON
END GRAIN

PLANE END GRAIN HALFWAY
FROM EACH EDGE TO
AVOID SPLITTING

How to Plane End Grain

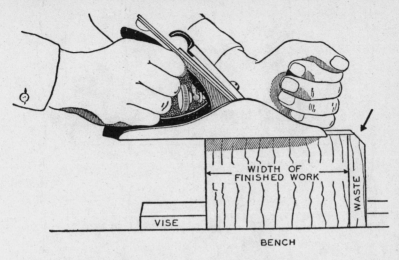

A Trick to Prevent Splitting End Grain

Use stock slightly wider than the finished work. Cut one corner off waste stock at a slight bevel. Plane end grain toward bevel. Then plane off waste stock.

planing. To plane a wood surface smooth, it is necessary to plane *with* the grain, *not against* it. If the wood is torn and roughened by a sharp plane set to make thin shavings, you are planing against the grain. Reverse the work and plane from the opposite end. If the grain is irregular, it may be necessary to plane one portion of a surface in one direction and the other portion in the opposite direction. When cross grain or curly grain is encountered, the plane iron must be very sharp and set to cut a very thin shaving.

It is necessary to plane *end* grain halfway from each edge. If you push a plane all the way across end grain, the corners and the edge will split off. You should never plane from the center to the corner on end grain. There are several "tricks" which can be used in end planing to avoid breaking corners at the end of the stroke. One of them is to use a wider piece of stock than the finished piece and cut the corner off slightly at a bevel, as shown in the illustration, in order to relieve pressure on the last wood fibers. After end planing, the edge can be planed to eliminate the bevel. Another method is to clamp a piece of wood on the edge of the board which is at the end of the plane stroke. This piece should be on the same level as the piece you are planing.

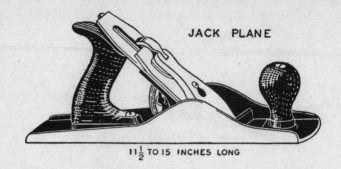

JACK PLANE

11½ TO 15 INCHES LONG

FORE PLANE

18 INCHES LONG

THE SMOOTHING, JACK, FORE AND JOINTER
PLANES ARE ALIKE EXCEPT IN LENGTH

You can hold the two pieces together either with the clamp
or in a vise.

The Jack, Fore, Smoothing, and Jointer Planes
The first few cuts on a long surface require a long plane. The bottom, called the sole, covers so much area that it rides over any hollows in the work and cuts only on the high spots until the surface is even.
Therefore it is easier to straighten a long edge or surface
with a long plane than with the shorter variety. After the

HOLLOW   HOLLOW

The long sole of the jack, fore and jointer planes rides over the
hollows in the work and cuts on the high spots.

roughness has been removed with a long plane, the work can be finished with a smaller plane called a *smoothing* plane.

Long planes are called jack, fore or jointer planes depending upon their length. The sole of a jack plane is usually from 11 1/2″ to 14″; the sole of a fore plane is 18″ and the sole of a jointer plane is 22″ or 24″. Among these three, the jack plane is used most often. Since all three are alike except for the length of sole, our discussion of a jack plane will apply equally well to the other two.

Planing with a Jack Plane. At the back of a jack plane is a handle somewhat like a saw handle. A knob is fixed to the front end. It is a tool to be used with two hands. The work must be secured so that it will not move while being planed. At the start of the planing stroke, take a position directly behind the work with the left foot forward. As you push the plane, shift the weight of the body gradually to the left foot. If the work being planed is long, it may be necessary to take one or two steps in order to finish the stroke.

Proper Adjustment of Plane Iron. The jack, smoothing, fore and jointer planes each has a plane iron cap clamped to the cutting blade. This has a double purpose. It stiffens the iron and breaks and curls the shavings as they come up through the throat. The breaking and curling and the action of the toe (this is the portion of the sole forward of the throat) prevent the wood from splitting ahead of the cutting edge and are the reasons for the cutting edge producing a smooth surface.

The position of the plane iron cap in relation to the plane iron is adjustable and can be shifted by loosening the clamping screw. A correct adjustment is essential. For general work, the edge of the plane iron cap should be about 1/16″ back of the cutting edge of the plane iron. It should be as near the cutting edge as possible when cross-grained or curly wood is to be planed.

The thickness of the shaving is adjusted by sighting along the bottom of the plane and turning the adjusting screw until the blade projects about the thickness of a hair. The blade is pushed out when the adjusting nut is turned so that it moves toward the handle. Turning the adjusting nut so that it moves in toward the blade draws the blade in and decreases the thickness of the shaving.

The plane must be set so that it makes a shaving of even thickness. This is done with the lateral adjusting lever. Sight along the bottom of the plane and move the lever to the right or left, whichever direction may be necessary in order to make the cutting edge parallel to the bottom.

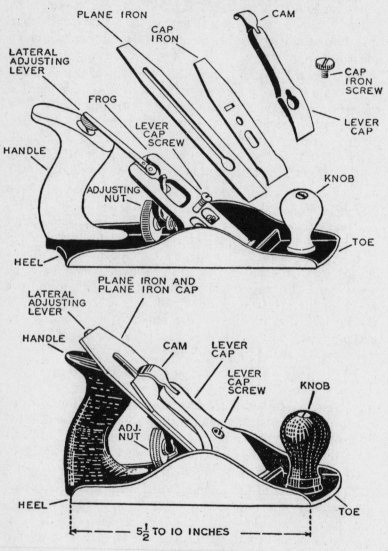

THE SMOOTHING PLANE

This is the shortest of the two-handed planes. It is used to smooth work after unevenness has been removed by a longer plane.

Smoothing Planes A smoothing plane is used to smooth the surface of work after the rough surface and unevenness have been removed with a jack plane. It is considerably larger than a block plane but smaller than a jack plane. It will not cut end grain as well as a block plane because the blade is set at a greater angle.

A smoothing plane is made exactly like a jack plane but has a shorter sole. This may be from 5 1/2" to 10" long.

A smoothing plane has a plane iron cap attached to the plane iron to curl and break the shavings. It has a handle and a knob and is used with two hands in the same manner as a jack plane. It should also be set in the same way. The edge of the plane iron cap should be about 1/16" back of the cutting edge of the plane iron for general work and as near to the cutting edge as possible for curly and cross-grained wood. The cutting edge of the plane iron should project about the thickness of a hair through the throat and be parallel to the bottom of the plane. This adjustment is made by sighting along the bottom of the plane and shifting the adjusting nut and lateral adjusting lever as may be necessary.

The cutting edge on the blade of a smoothing plane must be kept very sharp and be set to make a fairly fine shaving. If the throat of the plane becomes clogged, stop planing and

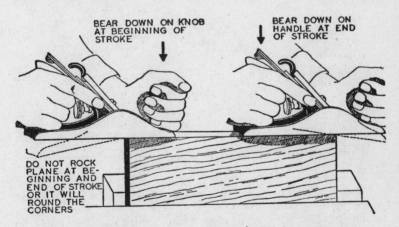

BEAR DOWN ON KNOB AT BEGINNING OF STROKE

BEAR DOWN ON HANDLE AT END OF STROKE

DO NOT ROCK PLANE AT BEGINNING AND END OF STROKE OR IT WILL ROUND THE CORNERS

How to Produce a Shaving of Approximately the Same Thickness from the Beginning to the End of the Stroke

clear it immediately. Use a wooden splint for this purpose. Never use a screw driver or anything made of metal because it will dull or nick the cutting edge if it is dragged across it.

Hold the plane as square as you can while you work and remember that since this plane has a short sole you can quickly make "hollows" and "rounds" with it if you do not apply the proper pressure to make an even shaving. At the beginning of any stroke, you should put a little more downward pressure on the knob with your left hand than you do on the handle with your right hand. When the stroke has been started, the pressure of both hands should be equal until toward the end. At the end, all the downward pressure should be exerted on the handle and practically none on the knob. This should result in a shaving of approximately the same thickness from the beginning to the end of the stroke.

It does not take much planing to dull a keen edge on a plane iron. You should be able to resharpen your own plane. Complete instructions for removing the blade, grinding and whetting it and putting the plane together again are given in Chapter 10.

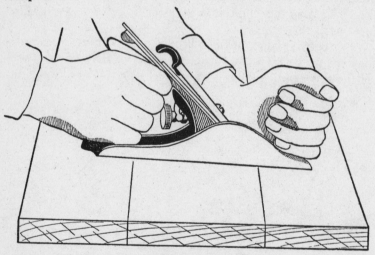

CROSS-PLANING

When a wide flat surface is made up of strips glued together or when wood is hard, curly-grained or cross-grained, it is easier to smooth it and true it by planing across grain. The plane must be very sharp and adjusted to make a very thin even shaving. The edge will dull more quickly than when planing with the grain. It should be kept sharp. Otherwise cross-planing produces a rough surface.

Roughing or Scrub Planes These tools are specially designed to save time and energy when it is necessary to remove a considerable amount of wood from a board—not enough to slice away with a rip saw but a great deal to plane away with a jack plane. They are made in two sizes—9 1/2″ long with a cutter 1 1/4″ wide and 10 1/2″ long with a cutter 1 1/2″ wide. The blade is heavy and rounded so that it will bring a board down to rough dimensions quickly. A smoothing plane or a jack plane can be used to finish the job if necessary.

A roughing or scrub plane is handled in the same manner as a jack plane. Carpenters frequently use it to back out base boards, clean up rough and gritty timbers, true up subflooring, bring large timbers to rough size, etc.

Special Low Angle Planes While a block plane does very nicely in cutting across the grain of ordinary boards and small or medium-sized pieces of wood, it is too small to work efficiently on timbers or other large pieces. When more power is required for cutting across the grain on heavy wood than can be applied to a regular block plane, a special low angle plane is used. This handles like a smoothing plane so that the power of both arms can be applied. The blade is set at a very low angle (12 degrees). A blade having a low angle cuts across hardwood more easily than a blade with a greater angle.

Edge Trimming Block Plane This is a time saver for the professional woodworker and a godsend to the amateur craftsman who has difficulty in planing square. The bottom of the plane consists of two surfaces at right angles. The cutter is at an angle so that it works on a skew. This plane will trim or square the edges of boards up to 7/8″ thick to a square or close fit without any effort required to keep the tool square with the edge. Wood blocks of various bevels may be attached to the bed of the plane so that accurate bevels can be planed on the edge of a board.

Model Maker's Plane. This is also known as a violin plane. It is a small tool, being only 3″ to 4″ long. The bottom is curved in both directions and the sharpened edge of the blade is rounded to conform with the curve of the bottom. The plane can be used to remove wood from any flat surface, from a convex surface of any radius and from con-

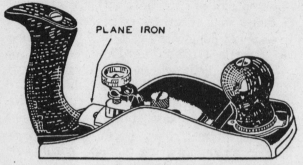

LOW ANGLE PLANE

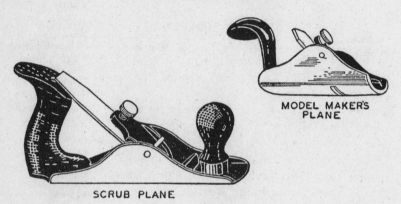

MODEL MAKER'S PLANE

SCRUB PLANE

EDGE-TRIMMING BLOCK PLANE

Special Planes

The low-angle plane cuts across grain more smoothly than the ordinary plane. The model maker's or violin plane has a curved sole and is used to shape and smooth both concave and convex surfaces. The scrub plane removes wood rapidly and is used to bring work down to rough dimensions. The edge-trimming block plane is used to trim and square the edge of boards.

cave surfaces down to those having a minimum radius of 12 inches.

Violin makers, pattern makers and professional model makers use this plane. Very few amateur craftsmen know that such a tool exists. It is not carried in stock in the average hardware store but can be procured upon order. Model boat builders will find it very useful.

Circular Planes　There are planes which will smooth a circular edge, either concave or convex. They are built with a flexible steel bottom which can be adjusted to form a curve so that concave and convex surfaces down to a minimum radius of 20 inches can be

WHEN PLANING AN EDGE HOLD FINGERS OF LEFT HAND ON BOTTOM AS A GUIDE

PLANING AN EDGE TRUE

Instead of holding the knob in the left hand, the hand is used as shown in the illustration. The thumb is placed on the iron frame just behind the knob and the fingers grasp the bottom of the plane. The finger tips rub lightly against the side of the board being planed so that any slight change in the angle of the plane can be detected and corrected. The sides of the plane must be kept parallel to the sides of the work.

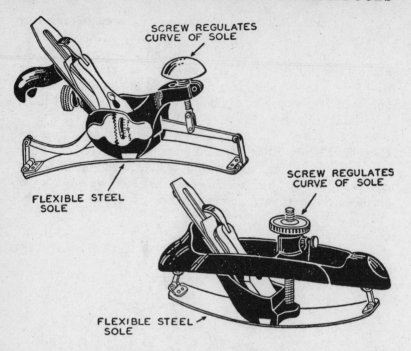

SCREW REGULATES
CURVE OF SOLE

FLEXIBLE STEEL
SOLE

SCREW REGULATES
CURVE OF SOLE

FLEXIBLE STEEL
SOLE

CIRCULAR PLANES FOR CURVED EDGES

planed. The same tool cannot be used for both convex and concave work.

Rabbet Planes. A rectangular recess cut out of the end or edge of a piece of wood is called a rabbet. Rabbets are used to form grooved joints in furniture, door, window and box construction and in other forms of woodwork. Rabbets can be cut by hand with a saw and chisel or planed with a special plane called a rabbet plane. The bottom of a rabbet plane is cut away so that the edge of the cutting iron is in line with the side of the plane. The illustration shows a simple type of bench rabbet plane and the rabbet which it forms. Short length rabbets across the end of a piece are usually cut with a saw and chisel, but if the rabbet plane is fitted with an iron called a spur it can be used to work across grain.

A rabbet plane is a two-handed tool, pushed in the same manner as a smoothing plane or jack plane.

The piece to be rabbeted should have a strip of wood clamped across it to act as a guide for the side of the plane.

The dotted lines in the piece in the illustration indicate the rabbet which is to be cut.

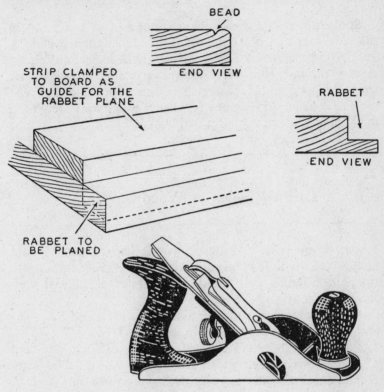

RABBET PLANE

Rabbet planes are used to work out square corners or laps. The cutting edge of the plane iron illustrated above is set at right angles to the side of the plane. The skew-iron type is set diagonally and cuts more easily and smoothly.

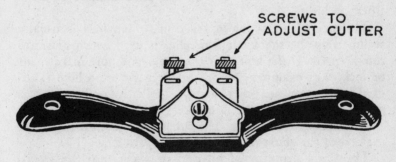

SPOKESHAVE FOR SHAPING AND SMOOTHING SMALL CURVES

A rabbet plane fitted with a properly shaped cutter is also used to cut the groove called a bead on the edge of woodwork.

Spoke Shaves. A spoke shave is not a plane but it cuts in the same way as a plane does and the blade is sharpened the same as a plane iron. It is held with both hands and pulled toward the operator. A spoke shave is a good tool to use for making a chamfer. Its principal use is for shaping curved pieces. It acquired its name because it was once widely used in shaping wooden wagon wheel spokes.

5   Drilling Holes in Wood

WHEN a hole is to be drilled in wood, the size, location and purpose of the hole determine whether an auger bit, expansion bit, Forstner bit, fluted drill, gimlet or a twist drill should be used.

Auger Bits. The common auger bits are sized by 1/16″ and are made in sizes to bore holes 1/4″, 5/16″, 3/8″, 7/16″, 1/2″, 9/16″, 5/8″, 11/16″, 3/4″, 13/16″, 7/8″, 15/16″ and 1″ in diameter. Holes which are smaller than 1/4″ in diameter are bored with a twist drill or double fluted drill. Small holes are also made with gimlet bits and bradawls. Small holes are bored mainly for wood screws. Although auger bits are made up to 2″ diameter, sizes larger than 1″ diameter are not common. Holes larger than 1″ diameter are therefore generally bored with an extension bit or a Forstner bit.

The size of an auger in fractions of an inch is usually stamped on the shank, or a number is used which indicates the diameter of the hole that the auger will bore in 16ths of an inch. For example, a No. 4 auger will bore a hole 4/16″ in diameter, or, in other words, 1/4″. A 5/16″ auger is marked 5; a 1/2″ auger is marked 8, and so on.

Differences in Augers. The cutting parts of an auger are the *screw*, the *spurs* or *nibs* and the *lips*.

The screw centers the bit and draws it into the wood. The screws have different pitches. They are made *fast,*

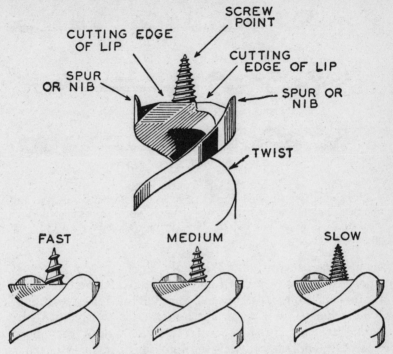

CUTTING EDGE
OF LIP

SCREW
POINT

CUTTING
EDGE OF LIP

SPUR
OR NIB

SPUR OR
NIB

TWIST

FAST   MEDIUM   SLOW

The Cutting End of an Auger Bit

The screw centers and draws the bit into the wood. The spurs or nibs score the circle and the lips cut out the wood. The pitch of the screw determines the cutting speed of the bit.

medium and *slow*. The fast pitch cuts fast and has a coarse thread. The slow pitch cuts slow and has a fine thread (see illustration). An auger bit with a screw having a medium pitch is most serviceable for all around work. Fast and medium screws work best in boring end wood or resinous wood because they do not clog up as easily as a fine-threaded screw. An auger bit with a slow thread bores the smoothest hole.

The spurs or nibs on the auger score the circumference of the hole and the lips cut the shavings. The twist or thread of the bit lifts the shavings out of the hole; it is a conveyor. Three types of auger bits whose differences lie in their threads will be found in general use in woodworking shops. They are called *single twist, double twist* and *straight core* or *solid-center* auger bits.

The single twist and straight core bore faster and clear

SINGLE SPUR CAR BIT OR SHIP AUGER

DOUBLE TWIST

SINGLE TWIST SOLID CENTER

TYPES OF AUGER BITS

The single twist is best for fast work and for hard and gummy woods. The double twist cuts more slowly and more smoothly and accurately. Ship augers and car bits are much longer than ordinary carpenters' augers.

themselves of chips more rapidly than the double twist type. They also bore *hard* and *gummy* woods better. They are the auger bits most generally used in the home workshop.

The double twist auger bit bores more slowly than one having a single thread but at the same time it cuts more accurately and smoothly. The hole which it bores is truer in size than the hole made by a single thread auger. It is best for boring *soft* woods. Cabinetmakers use the double twist.

Dowel Bits. These are short auger bits about one-half the length of ordinary auger bits. They are, as their name implies, used for drilling holes for dowel pins.

Ship Augers. These are auger bits from 18″ to 24″ in length. Some have no screw or spur. They are used to bore through thick timbers and through planks edgewise. They are also called car bits.

Gimlet Bits. These are gimlets with a square shank so as to fit a brace. They are used for boring holes ranging in size from 1/16″ to 3/8″ needed when screws are to be inserted in hardwood. The size varies by 32nds of an inch and is stamped on the tang.

Forstner Bits. These have no twist and neither screw nor spurs. The cutting is done by two lips and a circular steel rim. The rim centers the bit and scores the circle which forms the circumference of the hole bored by the bit. Forstner bits cut very accurately. They are made in sizes up to

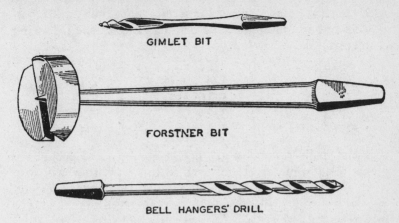

GIMLET BIT

FORSTNER BIT

BELL HANGERS' DRILL

Gimlet bits are used to bore screw holes. Forstner bits bore smoother, more accurate holes than an auger bit. Twist bits for wood resemble twist drills but are not tempered hard enough to cut metal. Bell hangers' drills, while designed for wood, will not be damaged by encountering metal.

2 inches in diameter. The sizes are indicated in 16ths of an inch and are stamped on the tang. Forstner bits have special uses and advantages over ordinary auger bits. These are:

1. They will bore well in end wood. An auger bit does not bore well in end wood.
2. They will bore a larger hole where a smaller hole has already been bored. This cannot be done with an auger bit without first plugging the smaller hole.
3. They will bore holes in thin wood near an end which the screw on an auger bit would split.
4. They will bore straight holes through knots and cross-grained wood.

Absence of a screw makes Forstner bits more difficult to center than auger bits. Centering them is made easier if a circle is drawn on the work with a pair of dividers equal to the size of the hole to be bored and located in the same place. The Forstner bit is started so that its rim coincides with the circumference of the circle. When boring holes completely through stock a piece of waste wood should be clamped to the back to prevent splitting as the bit cuts through.

Twist Drills for Wood and Metals. Twist drills for wood have a tapered shank to fit in a ratchet brace. They are

used to make holes in wood for screws, nails, bolts and small
dowels and are obtainable for drilling holes of the following
diameters:

1/16"	7/32"	1/2"
3/32"	1/4"	9/16"
1/8"	5/16"	5/8"
5/32"	3/8"	11/16"
3/16"	7/16"	3/4"

Twist drills *for wood* are not tempered hard enough to
make holes in metal. If misused in this way, they will lose
their sharp edges quickly and may be damaged severely.
Special bit stock drills, designed and tempered to make holes
in soft metal, which will fit into a ratchet brace, are often
used by woodworkers to make holes in both wood and soft
metal. These are especially useful in repair work where
hidden nails or unexpected metal may be encountered in
drilling into wood.

Boring Holes with Brace and Bit. It has been said that
there are two kinds of holes which can be bored in wood.
One kind is bored straight; it both goes in and comes out at
the intended place. The other is crooked, ending where it
is not supposed to.

Many a man who considers himself handy with tools
bores crooked holes. But it is easy to bore a hole which both
starts and ends where it should. It is merely necessary to
"sight" the auger or drill from two points 90 degrees apart.
One sight is made when beginning the hole and two more
after the hole is fairly well started. The auger will go
wherever it is sent. Sighting takes only a few seconds. The
method will be explained in a moment.

The Brace. A brace is a crank used to turn and guide
auger bits and drills. It can also be used as a powerful
screw driver. By placing a screw driver bit in the chuck
on the brace, screws can be driven or withdrawn with much
less physical exertion than would be required for the same
work done with a screw driver.

The best brace has a ball-bearing handle which makes
it easy to turn and a ratchet-driven chuck for holding the
bits. The ratchet may be locked or made to operate in
either direction. The ratchet makes it possible to use the
brace in confined spaces where there is not room enough to

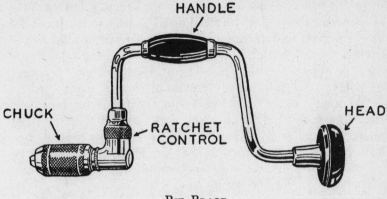

HANDLE

CHUCK

RATCHET
CONTROL

HEAD

BIT BRACE

turn the brace a full 360 degrees. A universal chuck which will hold all sizes of regular square shank bits, No. 1 Morse taper shank bits and round shanks from 1/8″ to 1/2″, is desirable. Prices of the various styles of braces vary with quality.

How to Use a Brace and Bit To use a brace and bit, first make certain that the chuck is screwed up tight. Then go to work. Hold the brace with the palm and fingers of the left hand and turn it with the right. Of course, if you are a southpaw you will find it more natural to reverse this position by holding the brace with your right hand and turn it with your left. At a bench it is usual to hold the brace and bit either vertically or horizontally, unless, of course, the hole is to be bored at an angle to the surface of the work. A vertical or horizontal position helps your eyes to more accurately sight the brace and bit at right angles to the surface of the piece which is to be bored.

When a hole is to be bored in wood, its exact center should be located on the work and marked with a bradawl. The point of the lead screw on the auger is placed in this mark. Then the handle of the brace is turned slowly in a clockwise direction, at the same time pressure is exerted on the head of the brace. The lead screw will bite into the wood the same as an ordinary wood screw. When hard woods are bored, it is necessary to apply more pressure to the head of the brace than is used when boring soft woods. The pressure of the hand and the pull of the lead screw both force the auger bit into the wood. As soon as the spurs (see sketch of auger bit) touch the work, the eyes are brought down to that level where the auger can be sighted from two positions 90 degrees apart to determine whether it is perpendicular to the surface of the work. Both sights cannot be made from the same position. Sighting from one position will show whether or not you are holding the auger bit perpendicular to the work in one plane; sighting from the other position will show the same thing with respect to another plane at right angles to the first. If the auger is not perpendicular in both planes, shift the position of the brace head until it is. Then hold the brace head steady, apply the proper amount of pressure and start boring.

If you are not sure of your eye, that is if you cannot judge

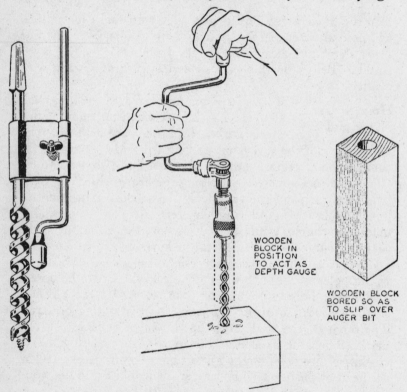

WOODEN BLOCK IN POSITION TO ACT AS DEPTH GAUGE

WOODEN BLOCK BORED SO AS TO SLIP OVER AUGER BIT

Depth Gauges for Boring Holes

There are gauges on the market but one can easily be made at home from a block of soft wood, bored so that it will slip over the auger bit. It is cut to proper length so that when it butts against the chuck the auger projects a distance equal to the hole to be bored.

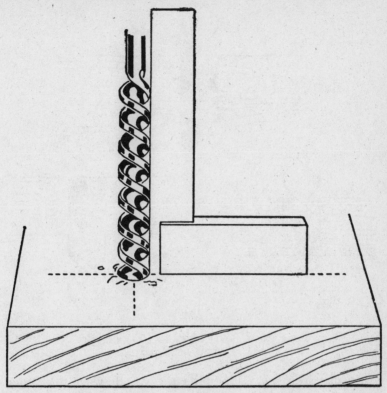

BORING PERPENDICULAR TO A SURFACE
Check the position of the auger with a try square until your eye
is trained.

a perpendicular accurately, test the position of the auger bit
in two planes with a small try square.

When the spurs and cutting edges of the auger bit have
started to bore into the wood, sight the work once more. If
the auger is still perpendicular in both planes continue boring
until it is near the bottom of the hole. At this point, turn
the brace slowly. Watch closely for the bottom of the lead
screw to come through the under side of the work. As soon
as it does, *stop* turning the brace. Remove all pressure from
the head of the brace and turn the handle slowly in the opposite direction (counterclockwise) so as to back out the
lead screw from the wood in which it is imbedded. Continue to turn the brace counterclockwise so as to withdraw
the auger as soon as the lead screw is free. Now turn the
work over and bore from the opposite side.

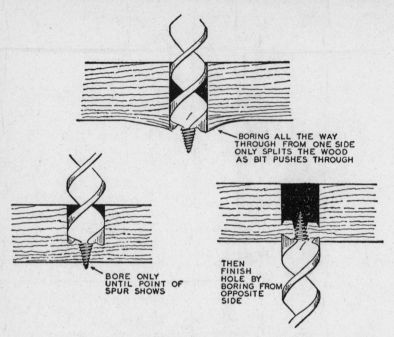

BORING ALL THE WAY
THROUGH FROM ONE SIDE
ONLY SPLITS THE WOOD
AS BIT PUSHES THROUGH

BORE ONLY
UNTIL POINT OF
SPUR SHOWS

THEN
FINISH
HOLE BY
BORING FROM
OPPOSITE
SIDE

BORE FROM BOTH SIDES TO PREVENT BIT
FROM BREAKING THROUGH

Boring from one side splits the wood when the auger
breaks through. Boring from two sides results in a smooth,
clean edged hole; if you have sighted the auger accurately,
the hole will have come through where you wanted it to.

You can bore from one side only, without danger of
splintering when the auger comes through, by clamping
a block of wood tightly on the back of the work in position
so that the auger will cut into it after it has completed the
hole in the work.

Boring at an Angle. Boring holes at a slight angle is no
more difficult than boring them at right angles to a surface.

Once upon a time a Tennessee mountaineer who was
trying to drive a Model T Ford for the first time, went off
the road, through a rail fence, cut a figure eight in the road-
side field and came to a stop with the front axle jammed tight
against a stump. He had just paid some hard-earned money
for the car, but did not seem a bit downcast over the damage
done to the radiator and front springs. "I found out something," he said, "they go right where you point 'em."

Like the Model T if you sight an auger or a drill at an angle, it will go where you aim it.

If the angle of the hole is only slightly away from the perpendicular or horizontal, there will be no difficulty in starting the auger and getting it to bite into the wood. It is a good plan to lay the angle out on a piece of thin wood or cardboard and use this in sighting. If the auger is kept parallel to the line indicating the angle, the drill will go where it should.

When a hole is to be bored at a considerable angle away from the perpendicular to a surface, it is difficult to start the auger without a guide. The guide is made by boring a vertical hole through a block of wood, using the same size auger bit that is to be used in making the finished hole. The bottom of the block is then sawed off at the proper angle and clamped or fastened with finishing nails to the work to be bored. The center of the hole in the bottom of the block must be directly over the starting point at the center of the hole about to be bored. Then if the auger is inserted in the hole in the block, you can bore the hole while the block holds the auger at the proper angle and prevents it from slipping.

It is easy to calculate the angle to be given the bottom of the block. Deduct from 90 the angle of the hole to be bored. The remainder is the number of degrees the angle of the bottom of the block should have. For example, if a hole is to be bored at an angle of 60 degrees, deduct 60 from 90 and the answer will be 30 degrees. Make the angle of the bottom of the block 30 degrees.

Extension or Expansive Bits   When holes larger than one inch in diameter are to be bored in wood, a carpenter or cabinetmaker employs an extension or

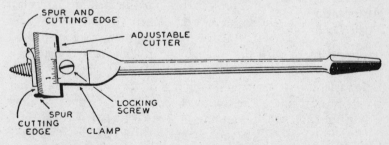

THE EXTENSION OR EXPANSIVE BIT CAN BE ADJUSTED
TO BORE HOLES OF ANY DIAMETER WITHIN ITS RANGE

expansive bit. This fits into a brace like an ordinary auger bit but has an adjustable cutting blade which can be set to bore holes of any diameter within its range. It is used in the same manner as the auger bit. Two sizes are made. The small size will produce holes from 1/2" to 1 1/2" in diameter. The large size makes holes 7/8" to 3" in diameter.

The spur and cutting lip is fastened to the shank by a screw passing through a small steel clamp. Loosening this screw makes it possible to move the spur and adjust the bit. The screw must be firmly tightened again so that the spur cannot slip while the hole is being bored. The accuracy of the adjustment should always be tested by boring a hole in a piece of waste wood and measuring its diameter. Not until this check has been made, should the bit be used to bore a hole in the finished work.

Boring through from one side only with an extension bit may split the wood. It is better to bore until the tip of the spur or lead screw appears on the under side. Then turn the work over and finish the hole by boring through from the opposite direction.

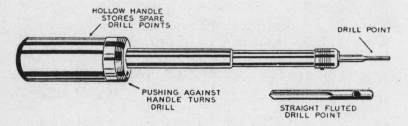

AUTOMATIC PUSH DRILL FOR STRAIGHT FLUTED DRILL POINTS

Automatic Push Drill
This tool speeds up the drilling of small holes in wood. When the handle is held with one hand and the sliding sleeve moved back and forth with the other hand, the chuck and drill will revolve. Carpenters use a push drill frequently to make holes for screws used in fastening hinges, locks and other hardware fittings. The hollow handle usually contains a set of straight flute drills ranging in size from 1/16" to 11/64".

Countersink Bit
This tool is used to shape the top of a screw hole so that the head of a flat head screw may be driven flush with, or slightly

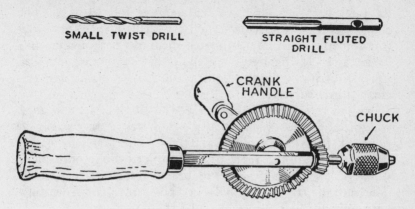

SMALL TWIST DRILL STRAIGHT FLUTED DRILL

CRANK HANDLE CHUCK

HAND DRILL
For driving small twist drills and straight fluted drills.

below, the surface of the work. There are two types. One has a tapered shank to fit a bit brace; the other has a straight round shank to fit a hand drill.

The Hand Drill   When small diameter, accurate holes are to be drilled in wood, Morse twist drills are used. These are made with a straight shank and may be driven by a hand drill or an electric drill. Power driven drills are used for high-speed production. The 3-jaw chuck with which the ordinary hand drill is fitted takes drills up to 1/4″ in diameter. To drive twist drills of larger diameter by hand, a breast drill should be used. The chuck on this tool will usually take straight shank drills up to 1/2″ in diameter.

When drilling with a Morse twist drill it is necessary to hold the driving mechanism steady and drive the drill perfectly straight. Otherwise the drill may be bent or broken. The shank of the drill is soft and will bend but the body of the drill is tempered and will break if sufficiently strained.

When driven rapidly, a small twist drill will bite into wood very fast but if it is pushed ahead too quickly, the chips will not clear out properly. When this occurs, the drill becomes hot. If the wood is hard and the chips clog in the drill flutes, the drill may break or may become hot enough to char the wood and spoil its own temper. A burnt twist drill will no longer hold a keen cutting edge.

Withdraw the drill several times to clear the chips from

its flutes before a hole in hard wood is fully drilled. The chips will usually fall out when the drill is withdrawn but it is sometimes necessary to push them out with a small nail or an awl. If the flutes are jammed with chips, the drill squeaks as it revolves. The drill should be withdrawn and cleared immediately.

Morse twist drills (see page 186 for sizes) are especially useful whenever a good job of setting a screw is to be done. Two drills are necessary then. The first part of the hole is drilled to the depth of the length of the smooth shank of the screw with a drill of the same diameter as that shank. The second part of the hole is made with a drill which is smaller than the threaded part of the screw.

Breast Drills. These are larger and more strongly built editions of the hand drill. The chuck will usually take straight shank drills up to 3/8" in diameter and sometimes will receive a 1/2" diameter drill. Breast drills are fitted with a plate instead of a handle. The chest or abdomen of the operator pressing against this plate provides the pressure which feeds the drill. Two sets of driving gears make it possible to change the speed ratio by shifting the spindle of the driving wheel to which the crank is attached.

Sharpening Auger Bits   An auger bit will usually bore a great many holes before it loses its keen cutting edge. When it will no longer bore easily or make a clean hole, it must be resharpened. Instructions for doing this will be found in Chapter 10.

---

6   Wood Chisels and How to Use Them

THERE are chisels for cutting wood and chisels for cutting metal. Chisels for cutting metals are called cold chisels. Their use is described in another chapter. Woodworking chisels cannot be used to cut metal and cold chisels are of no value as woodcutting tools.

The chisel is one of the most important and most used woodworking tools. It is indispensable in the construction of

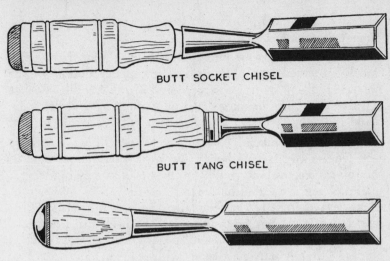

BUTT SOCKET CHISEL

BUTT TANG CHISEL

EVERLASTING CHISEL

THE THREE COMMON TYPES OF WOOD CHISELS

The blades are similar but the handle construction is different.
Socket and Everlasting chisels can be driven with a mallet or hammer. Tang chisels are intended to be driven by the pressure of the
hand only.

most wood joints made by hand. The modern woodworker's
chisel is a tapered steel blade forged from special chisel
steel and heat-treated to hold a keen cutting edge. One side
of the blade is flat; the other is beveled to meet the flat side
and form a cutting edge. Chisels are used so frequently in
hand woodworking that only the best quality should be purchased.

Although chisels for woodworking are made in many
sizes and shapes to suit the work they are to perform, they
may be divided into three general classes, known as tang,
socket and everlasting chisels.

Tang Chisels. The blade of a tang chisel is tapered to a
projecting shank called a tang and forced into a wood handle
or inserted in a molded plastic handle. The handle is re-
inforced against splitting by a metal ferrule and may have a
leather tip. Tang chisels are designed for carving, paring
and other light work. They are not built to withstand the
blows of a heavy mallet or a steel hammer. They may be
driven with a light wooden or composition mallet without
danger of splitting the handle, but primarily they are in-

tended only for work in which they are driven by the pressure of the hand.

Socket Chisels. One end of the steel blade of a socket chisel is formed into a funnel-shaped socket that fits over the tapered end of a wood or composition handle. Socket chisels are of heavier construction than tang chisels. The blade is thicker. They can be driven with a heavy mallet.

Everlasting Chisels. Many carpenters and woodworkers who work away from a bench and must carry their tools to the job save space and weight in their tool kits by omitting a mallet. They use a nail hammer to drive chisels. It takes a great deal of force to cut vertically into such woods as yellow pine and oak. Driving a tang or socket chisel with a hammer will eventually spoil the handle. An everlasting chisel is made so that it may be driven with a steel hammer. The head of the handle where the hammer strikes, the shank, ferrule and blade are all one piece of steel so that a blow struck on the head is transmitted directly to the cutting edge of the blade.

Other Chisels. Differences in the length and thickness of the blade give chisels special qualities which make one better adapted to certain work than another. Consequently there are several varieties of chisels known as paring, butt, firmer, framing, pocket and mortise chisels whose differences lie in the proportions of their blades. Any variety of chisel may have either straight edges or beveled edges.

The Beveled-edge Chisel. The beveled-edge chisel is the preferred one. It is lighter and will reach into angles and under projections which are difficult to reach with a square-edged tool.

The Paring Chisel. The blade of a paring chisel is lighter and thinner than the blade of other chisels. It is used mainly for hand chiseling or paring.

The Firmer Chisel. The firmer chisel has a long, strong blade which makes it adaptable for both heavy and light work.

The Butt Chisel. The butt chisel is different from other chisels only in that it has a shorter blade (usually 2 1/2″ to 3″ long when new) and consequently can be used in places inaccessible to a longer blade.

The Mortise Chisel. The mortise chisel is used for chiseling mortises and consequently must be driven with a hammer or mallet. In chiseling a mortise the blade is used not only for cutting but also as a lever to force the chips out. Since it receives hard use the blade of a mortise chisel is made thick and strong just below the handle. If a mortise is first bored so that most of the wood is removed with an auger, it may be cleaned out and squared up with an ordinary firmer chisel. In that case a special mortise chisel is unnecessary.

Experience will soon teach the workman the most convenient size of chisel to use on a particular job. The chisel should always be smaller than the job. For example, in chiseling a recess 1″ wide in a piece of wood, the chisel used should not be 1″ wide; a 3/8″ or a 1/2″ chisel is the proper tool. The reason is that in general a chisel should not be pushed straight forward but moved laterally at the same time that it is pushed forward.

Chisel Sizes. All varieties of chisels are made with blades

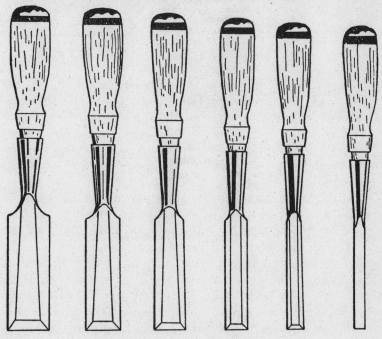

A SET OF CHISELS

A set of six chisels with blades varying in width from ⅛″ to 1½″ is the most useful assortment for general purposes.

varying from 1/8″ to 1″ in steps of 1/8″ and from 1″ to 2″ in steps of 1/4″. For most purposes the 1/4″, 1/2″, 3/4″ and 1″ widths suffice. A collection of nine or ten chisels which includes two or three paring chisels and six or seven firmer chisels is all that most professional woodworkers need and should satisfy the most particular amateur craftsman. Blade widths from 1/8″ to 1 1/2″ are the most useful for general purposes.

Glazier's Chisel. The carpenter or glazier uses this tool for loosening window sashes that stick, cleaning out old putty and smoothing sash for glass. The blade is usually about 3 1/4″ to 3 1/2″ long and 1 3/4″ to 2″ wide. The sides of the blade are not beveled. It is better to have a chisel especially for this work if only to avoid spoiling the keen edge or breaking the blade of a regular paring or butt chisel.

GLAZIER'S CHISEL FOR WORKING ON WINDOW SASH

How to Use a Chisel   You do not gain time by making haste with a chisel. There is always danger of unintentionally splitting the work if you take too large a cut. Whenever possible, other tools such as saws, planes and augers should be used to remove as much of the waste wood as possible and the chisel employed for finishing purposes only. This saves time and effort.

On rough work, the power which drives a chisel is usually the blow of a hammer or mallet. On fine work the driving power is applied entirely with the right hand. Most of the control is exercised by the left hand.

It is probably easier to cut yourself accidentally with a chisel than with any other tool, and the cut of a chisel can be wicked. The best safeguard against injury is to *hold the tool properly. Keep both hands back of the cutting edge at all times.* A safety precaution which will not only help to protect the mechanic but also make the work easier is *always secure the work* which is to be chiseled so that *it cannot move.*

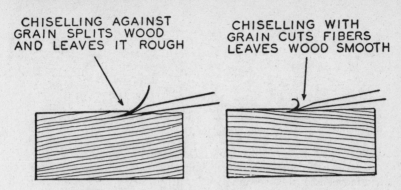

CHISELLING AGAINST GRAIN SPLITS WOOD AND LEAVES IT ROUGH

CHISELLING WITH GRAIN CUTS FIBERS LEAVES WOOD SMOOTH

CHISEL WITH THE GRAIN TO AVOID SPLITTING

When starting a cut with a chisel always cut away from the guide line and toward the waste wood so that any splitting which takes place will occur in the waste and not in the finished work. Do not start *on* the guide line. Start slightly away from it, so that there is a small amount of material to be removed by the finishing cuts. Never cut toward yourself with a chisel.

Make the shavings thin, especially when finishing. Examine the grain of the wood to see which way it runs. Cut with the grain. This severs the fibers and leaves the wood smooth. Cutting against the grain splits the fibers and leaves the wood rough. Such a cut cannot be controlled.

Chiseling may be done by cutting either horizontally or vertically. Vertical chiseling cuts are usually made across grain.

Horizontal Chiseling **Paring.** If the cutting edge of a sharp chisel is examined under a magnifying glass, it will appear saw-toothed. If the chisel is slanted slightly in the direction of the cut, the minute teeth will cut more easily and smoothly. This gives a shearing cut which should be used whenever possible, both with the grain and on end grain. Cutting *fine* shavings with a shearing cut is called *paring.*

To Cut Horizontally with the Grain. The chisel handle is grasped in the right hand with the thumb extended toward the blade. The cut is controlled by holding the blade firmly with the left hand, knuckles up and the hand well back of the cutting edge. The right hand is used to force the chisel into the wood and push it away from the work. The left

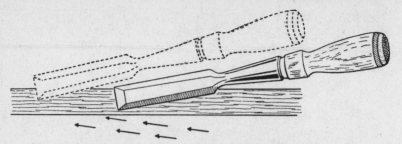

A Shearing Cut Is Used When Possible

The chisel should be slanted slightly in the direction of the cut and moved slightly sideways as it is pushed forward. The illustration shows a chisel at the start of a horizontal cut. The dotted lines indicate the position of the chisel toward the end of the cut and show that the tool has been moved slightly sideways at the same time it was pushed forward, thus making a shearing cut.

hand pressing downward on the chisel blade regulates the length and depth of the cut. For a roughing cut hold the chisel with the bevel down. To make a finishing cut, work with the bevel up.

As already explained the chisel cuts more easily and leaves a smoother surface when the cutting edge is held at a slight diagonal to the direction of the cut or is given a slight sliding motion. This can be done by holding the tool so that it is turned a bit to one side as it is pushed forward or by moving it slightly from left to right at the same time that it is advanced.

The cutting edge of a chisel tends to follow the direction of the wood fibers. The cut cannot be controlled in chiseling

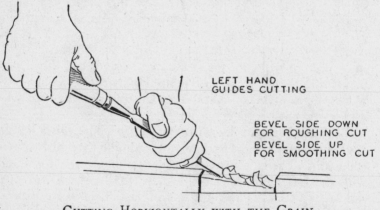

LEFT HAND
GUIDES CUTTING

BEVEL SIDE DOWN
FOR ROUGHING CUT
BEVEL SIDE UP
FOR SMOOTHING CUT

Cutting Horizontally with the Grain

against the grain. There is danger of splitting and damaging the work. Consequently a chisel cut should *always* be made with the grain. With cross-grained wood it is necessary to work from both directions so as to cut only with the grain.

Remember, chiseling should not be hurried and only fine shavings should be cut. If thick shavings are cut the tool may dig in and split off a piece of wood which was never intended to be cut.

Chamfering with a Chisel. A chamfer is made by flattening the sharp corner between two surfaces which are at right angles to each other. A plain chamfer runs the full length of the edge and is usually made with a plane. A stopped chamfer does not run the full length of the edge. If a stopped chamfer is long enough, part of it can be planed and the ends finished with a chisel. A short stopped chamfer must be made entirely with a chisel. A chamfer is usually made at 45 degrees. Guide lines which mark its edges should be made with a pencil. In the case of a 45 degree chamfer the guide lines will be the same distance back from the edges on both surfaces. A marking gauge, scratch awl or penknife should not be used to make the guide lines for a chamfer because they produce marks in the wood which are difficult to remove.

To cut a stopped chamfer hold the chisel with the edge parallel to the slope of the chamfer and cut with the grain as in ordinary horizontal paring. Begin chiseling at the ends and work toward the center. The ends of the chamfer may be either flat or curved. If flat, use the chisel with the bevel up. If curved, work with the bevel down. Unless the grain of the wood is quite straight, there is some danger of splitting off too much wood if a roughing cut is used. Rather than risk spoiling the work, it is better for the novice to use light smoothing entirely, holding the chisel diagonally, even if this does take more time to remove the surplus stock. The experienced mechanic can often safely remove most of the surplus wood from the chamfer with roughing cuts and then finish with smoothing cuts.

To Cut Diagonally across the Grain. To cut a straight slanting corner, as shown in the illustration, as much waste wood as possible is first removed with a saw. The work is then clamped in a bench vise with the guide line horizontal and the chisel used in the same manner as in horizontal chiseling with the grain. Here again it is necessary to chisel with the grain and to hold the chisel so that the cutting edge is slightly diagonal to the direction of the cut.

To Chisel a Round Corner. To cut a round corner on the end of a piece of wood, first lay out the work, then re-

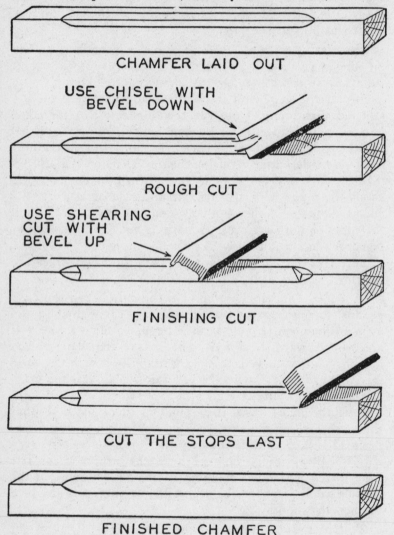

CHAMFER LAID OUT

USE CHISEL WITH
BEVEL DOWN

ROUGH CUT

USE SHEARING
CUT WITH
BEVEL UP

FINISHING CUT

CUT THE STOPS LAST

FINISHED CHAMFER

CUTTING A STOPPED CHAMFER WITH A CHISEL

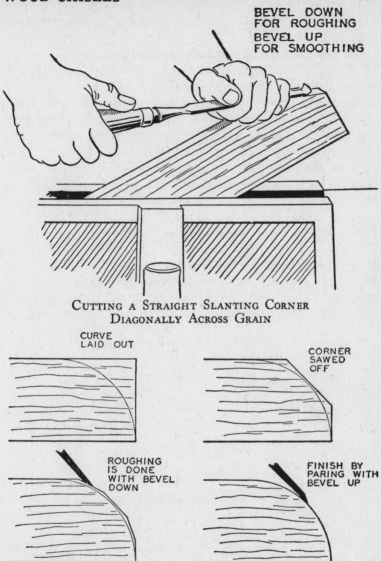

BEVEL DOWN
FOR ROUGHING
BEVEL UP
FOR SMOOTHING

CUTTING A STRAIGHT SLANTING CORNER
DIAGONALLY ACROSS GRAIN

CURVE
LAID OUT

CORNER
SAWED
OFF

ROUGHING
IS DONE
WITH BEVEL
DOWN

FINISH BY
PARING WITH
BEVEL UP

THE STEPS IN CHISELING A ROUND CORNER

move as much of the waste as possible with a saw. Use a
chisel with the bevel down to make a series of straight cuts
tangent to the curve. In making these cuts the chisel is
moved sideways across the work at the same time that it is
moved forward. The curve is finished by paring with the
beveled side of the chisel up.

Convex Curves are chiselled in the same manner as a round corner.

To Cut Horizontally across Grain. To make any of the lap joints in woodworking, the wood between the saw cuts is removed with a chisel. This calls for cutting horizontally across the grain of the wood. The work should be held in a vise. Most of the waste wood is removed by the chisel with the bevel held down. On light work the pressure of the hand or light blows on the end of the chisel handle with the palm of the right hand will provide sufficient driving force. On heavier work a mallet must be used. To avoid splitting at the edges, cut from each edge to the center and slightly upward so that the waste stock at the center is removed last.

The finishing cuts are made with the flat side of the chisel down. A mallet should not be used in making the finishing cuts, even on large work. The pressure of the right hand is all that is required to drive the chisel which is guided by the thumb and forefinger of the left hand. The thumb and forefinger act as a brace and also give the chisel a sideways

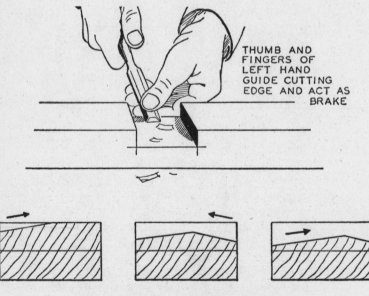

THUMB AND
FINGERS OF
LEFT HAND
GUIDE CUTTING
EDGE AND ACT AS
BRAKE

TO AVOID SPLINTERING CORNERS
WHEN CHISELLING ACROSS GRAIN CUT
HALFWAY FROM EACH EDGE TOWARD CENTER

CHISELING HORIZONTALLY ACROSS GRAIN

paring motion as it is pushed forward. The finishing cuts should also be made from each edge toward the center. Do not cut all the way across from one edge or the far edge may be split off.

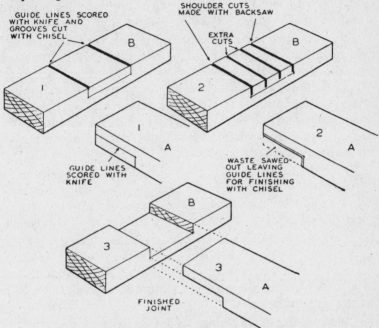

MAKING A HALF LAP JOINT
WILL PROVIDE EXERCISE IN CHISELING

Chiseling Practice As an exercise for gaining skill in the free use of chisels there is nothing better than making a few lap joints. The simple half-lap or middle-lap joint shown in the illustration is a good starting point for the beginner. White pine is the best material to use in the beginning. When a perfect joint can be made in white pine, the novice should test his workmanship on other woods with coarser grain.

The first operation is to cut a groove on the waste side of the knife cuts which are the guide lines for the shoulders of the joint. The grooves should be cut with the beveled side of the chisel up. The shoulders of the joint are cut down almost to the horizontal guide line with a backsaw. The saw is started in the grooves which help produce a straight cut. A few extra saw cuts made between the shoulder cuts and without the aid of starting grooves will make the chiseling out of the waste stock easier and prevent material from splitting off below the horizontal or depth guide line. The waste material is cut away with the chisel held bevel down. Work from both sides to avoid splitting wood off at the edges. Take only light cuts.

The joints are finished by paring with a very sharp chisel held bevel up and with the flat side of the chisel in contact with the wood. Only very light cuts are taken. When both parts of the joint are pared down to the guide line they are fitted together and checked. Any irregularities or high spots are removed with the chisel. The two parts should fit together firmly and snugly. It should not be necessary to force them together.

The beginner should continue to make these joints until he can do so accurately and easily. Then some dovetail joints should be attempted. The mechanic who can make good dovetail joints is no longer a novice with the chisel.

Vertical Chiseling　　Vertical chiseling means cutting at right angles to the surface of the wood. Usually it involves cutting across the wood fibers as in chiseling out the ends of a mortise or making a gain or stopped dado joint.

When vertically chiseling across grain a mallet may be used to drive the chisel. If the wood is maple or other hardwood, a mallet is necessary. But if the edge is with the grain, to drive the chisel with a mallet is to risk splitting the wood. A shearing cut is the only one that will probably make much progress in cutting across grain. The chisel should be brought from a position slightly to one side of vertical to vertical as it is driven down, or, the cutting edge should be slid to one side as it is pressed down. Either method will produce a shearing cut.

To Cut a Concave Curve. In cutting a concave curve, it may be possible to conserve time and effort by removing most of the waste wood with a coping saw or a compass saw. Smooth and finish the curve by chiseling. The chiseling must be with the grain. The left hand is used to hold the bevel side of the chisel against the work. The right hand should press down on the chisel and at the same time draw back on the handle to drive the cutting edge in a sweeping curve. It

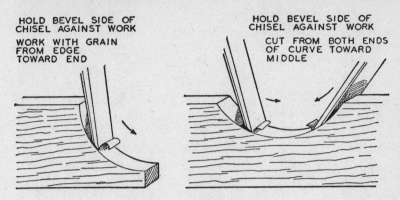

HOLD BEVEL SIDE OF
CHISEL AGAINST WORK

WORK WITH GRAIN
FROM EDGE
TOWARD END

HOLD BEVEL SIDE OF
CHISEL AGAINST WORK

CUT FROM BOTH ENDS
OF CURVE TOWARD
MIDDLE

CHISELING CONCAVE CURVES

Hold chisel blade against work with the left hand. Drive chisel with pressure of right hand on handle.

is difficult to control the depth in this sort of cut. Care must be used to take only light cuts.

To Cut Vertically across Grain. The work should be clamped or otherwise secured so that it cannot move under the pressure of chiseling. If care is used, much of the waste wood can be removed by driving the chisel with a mallet. Vertical chiseling which can be carried to the workbench should be done with a cutting board or bench hook between the work and the bench, never directly on the bench top. Then the cutting edge of the chisel will not mar the bench at the end of its stroke.

A shearing cut should be used in cutting vertically across the grain. Always cut with the grain so that the waste wood will split *away* from the guide marks. If part of the chisel is kept pressed against the portion just cut, it will guide that part of the chisel cutting a new portion of the surface.

Vertical Chiseling on End Wood. Use a bench hook or cutting board under the work. Remove as much waste wood as possible with a saw. Observe the direction of the grain and start to cut at an edge to avoid splitting the wood. Use a shearing cut and make the shavings thin. Thin shavings can be made without the aid of a mallet. Grasp the handle of the chisel in the right hand with the thumb pressing down on the top of the handle. Use the left hand to guide the tool, and to supply some of the driving force if much pressure is needed.

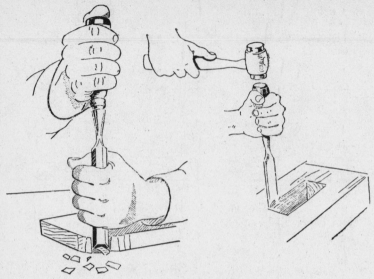

VERTICAL CHISELING

Vertical chiseling usually means cutting at right angles to the surface of the wood and across the fibers. On end wood, work from the edge toward the end or with the grain. Some vertical chiseling can be done without a mallet but frequently one is necessary.

Gouges
A gouge is a chisel with a concave blade which gives it a curved cutting edge. Firmer gouges are ground with the bevel either on the outside or the inside. Paring gouges are ground with the bevel on the inside only. The curve of a paring gouge is flatter than the curve of a firmer gouge and may be had in three styles, called the flat sweep, medium sweep and regular sweep in widths from 1/8" to 2".

Gouges are used for cutting hollows and grooves, shaping core boxes (used in foundry work) and paring the ends of irregular surfaces which must be matched together. A gouge with an inside bevel is handled in the same way as a chisel with the bevel up. A gouge with an outside bevel is used in the same manner as a chisel with the bevel down.

A gouge is always started at the edge of a cut and driven toward the center. In gouging out a large hollow, the depth of each cut can be kept under better control if the cutting is done across grain.

A bent-shank gouge is used to cut a long groove. The bent shank raises the handle clear of the work. This gouge

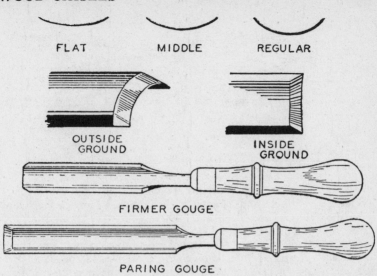

FLAT   MIDDLE   REGULAR

OUTSIDE
GROUND

INSIDE
GROUND

FIRMER GOUGE

PARING GOUGE

GOUGES ARE CHISELS WITH CURVED CUTTING EDGES

The curve of the edge may be either a flat, medium or regular sweep as illustrated above. Paring gouges are inside ground, have tang handles and are used to cut the ends of moldings, etc. Firmer gouges may be either inside or outside ground and have either a tang or socket handle. They are for cutting hollows and grooves.

can be used at a very low angle to the work surface and allow room for the fingers under the handle.

Woodcarving Woodcarving is one of the great arts. Men devote a lifetime to it and it is too large a subject to more than mention in this book. When roughing out large work the woodcarver sometimes uses the chisels and gouges, etc. of the carpenter but for the actual carving, he has special tools called carving tools. These are chisels and gouges which differ from the ordinary in that the blades taper toward the tang instead of having parallel sides and surfaces. The taper gives them clearance back of the cutting edge. There are many different sizes and shapes of carving tools. The cutting edge of the chisels may be either square or oblique with the blade and the blade may be straight or bent. The carving gouges are made with eleven different sweeps or curves. The V-shaped carving gouges are called parting tools and the narrow, deep, U-shaped gouges are known as veiners. The larger deep gouges are fluters and those with a flat curve are called flats.

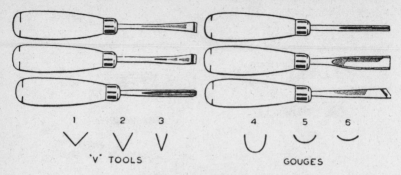

CARVING TOOLS

These are chisels and gouges made especially for carving low relief designs, small models, etc. Their edges are ground at the factory but should be whetted on a fine oilstone before being used. Carving tools must have keen edges to be fully useful. The three "V" tools illustrated are known as 1. obtuse, 2. medium and 3. acute. The gouges are called 1. quick, 2. medium and 3. flat.

The handle of small carving tools is ball shaped and made to fit in the palm of the hand. The blade is grasped between the thumb and forefinger.

The average craftsman desiring to carve small models or simple designs in low relief needs only a small assortment of carving tools. The most important are illustrated. A keen razorlike edge should be maintained on all carving tools by frequently honing them on an oil slip stone. It is necessary to observe the grain of the work and to cut insofar as is possible only with the grain.

When carving a design such as a low relief, the design is

WOOD FILE

WOOD RASP

FILES AND RASPS FOR WOODWORKING

The use of files and rasps in woodworking is not recommended except where it is impractical or impossible to use a cutting tool. Wood rasps cut faster but leave a rougher surface than wood files.

outlined on the wood with pencil. The first cutting is done with a parting tool or a small gouge by making a shallow cut along the background side of the outline of the design. The background is then cut down with a flat gouge and whatever other tools may be necessary to conform to the design. The surface of the design is modeled and shaped with whatever tools are necessary in order to follow the form. A little experience will soon give the novice judgment in selecting the proper tools to use in the various stages of the carving. There are many books devoted wholly to the subject of woodcarving and anyone who desires to go deeply into the subject will find them informative and helpful.

---

7   Laying-out and Checking Operations

CUTTING wood to *exact* dimension is the basis of all good woodworking. Chisels, planes, saws, etc., are only a means to this end. Before any accurate cutting process can be undertaken successfully, guiding lines must be marked upon

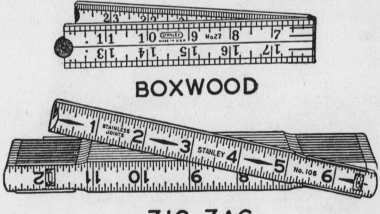

BOXWOOD

ZIG-ZAG   *Courtesy Stanley Tools*

STANDARD FOLDING RULES

The rules used by woodworkers are generally made of wood and fold into 6" lengths so that they can be carried in the pocket. The folding zig-zag type usually opens to 6' and the boxwood to 2' or 3'.

the work. The plan and measurements for the work may be taken from a blueprint or sketch or they may exist only in the mind of the workman. But in either case, a full-sized reproduction of the various angles, curves and details of the plan must be marked on the lumber which is the raw material. This measuring and marking process is called laying-out or setting-out. It is absolutely essential to a good piece of work. In an industrial woodworking plant, it is usually performed by the foremen and assistant foremen.

The tools used for laying out are rules, squares, gauges, dividers, pencils, knife blades and sliding T bevels.

Measuring Tools   Rules. The rules used by woodworkers are usually of the folding type so that they can be carried in a pocket. They are from 2' to 8' long and are usually graduated to show feet, inches and fractions of inches on both sides. They are also available with inch divisions on one side and metric divisions on the other.

Caliper Rule. This handy tool will measure the diameter of dowels, drills, and the thickness of boards, tenons, etc., more accurately than an ordinary rule. Some caliper rules are made for both inside and outside calipering. They can therefore be used to measure accurately the diameter of holes, the width of slots, etc.

Using a Rule. The joints of a folding rule should be lubricated with light machine oil occasionally to prevent rust and stiff joints which might break when the rule is opened or closed.

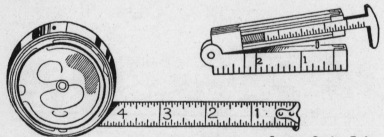

Courtesy Stanley Tools

STEEL TAPE AND CALIPER RULE

Pull-push steel tape rules have a steel blade that is rigid for measuring straight distances and becomes flexible under slight pressure so it can be used for measuring cylinders, curves and angular shapes. A caliper rule will measure thicknesses and diameters within its range more accurately than an ordinary rule.

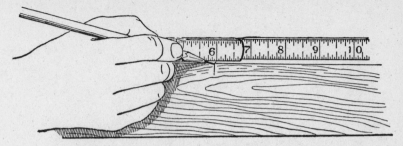

A RULE IS HELD ON EDGE FOR ACCURATE MEASUREMENTS

To measure distances of more than 2' the rule is laid flat on the surface to be measured. When a folding rule is laid on a flat surface, the rule itself is flat and therefore accurate. It is inaccurate to measure any great length with a folding rule held on edge. Since the rule is flexible, to hold it perfectly straight in this position is difficult.

When laying out accurate measurements of less than 2', the rule is placed on edge and the distance marked with a fine pencil point or the tip of a penknife blade.

Rules which have been used considerably are sometimes worn at the ends. It may be more accurate to measure from the 1-inch mark of an old rule instead of from the end.

Dividers. This tool is sometimes called a compass. Its principal use is to scribe small circles. It is also a handy instrument for picking up a measurement and transferring it to the work. For example, suppose it is necessary to lay out a number of lines 3" apart on a piece of board. If the dividers are set to 3" and are used to locate the lines, the distances between them will all be equal.

Squares   **Carpenter's Square.** The carpenter's steel square usually measures 24" x 16" or 24" x 18". The 24" side is called the body and the 16" or 18" side, at right angles to the body, is called the tongue. The flat sides of the body and tongue are graduated in inches and fractions of an inch. Both the body and tongue may be used as a rule and also as a straight edge.

Besides the inch and fractional graduations on the square, the following tables are marked on it: rafter or framing table, board measure, octagon scale, brace measure and hundredths scale. The square is as important a tool to the carpenter, as the slide rule is to the engineer. He performs

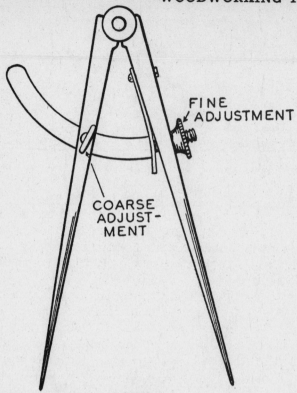

FINE ADJUSTMENT

COARSE ADJUST-MENT

DIVIDERS

Used for laying out circles or parts of circles and for picking up distances to be transferred to work.

many of his calculations with the aid of the graduations and tables marked on its sides and uses it to lay out the guide lines for cutting rafters, oblique joints, stairs, etc. In fact, the housebuilder employs the square in so many ways that whole books are devoted to its uses.

The cabinetmaker, jointer and amateur craftsman has little or no use for the tables on a carpenter's square or some of its special applications. They use it for laying out and squaring up large stock and large patterns and for testing the flatness and squareness of large surfaces. In their hands, it is handled much like its smaller brother, the try square.

Try Squares. The common try square consists of two parts at right angles to each other, a thick wood or iron stock and a thin steel blade. The best try squares are made with the blades graduated in inches and fractions of an inch. The blade length varies from 2" to 12".

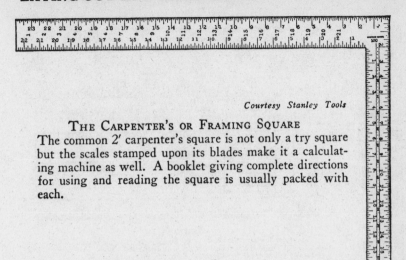

Courtesy Stanley Tools

THE CARPENTER'S OR FRAMING SQUARE

The common 2′ carpenter's square is not only a try square but the scales stamped upon its blades make it a calculating machine as well. A booklet giving complete directions for using and reading the square is usually packed with each.

A more convenient but slightly more expensive form of try square is the adjustable type whose blade can be locked in its seat at any point along its length. The iron stock is provided with a level.

A try square is a necessity in the woodworker's tool kit. It is used constantly for laying-out and to determine whether edges and ends are true with adjoining edges and with the

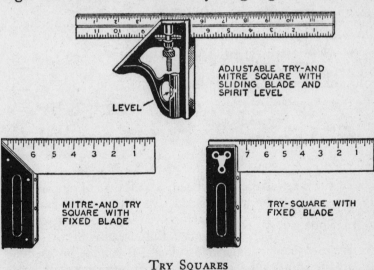

LEVEL

ADJUSTABLE TRY-AND MITRE SQUARE WITH SLIDING BLADE AND SPIRIT LEVEL

MITRE-AND TRY SQUARE WITH FIXED BLADE

TRY-SQUARE WITH FIXED BLADE

TRY SQUARES

The try square is used for testing surfaces and laying out lines at 90° to each other. The miter square may be used for 45° and 90° work.

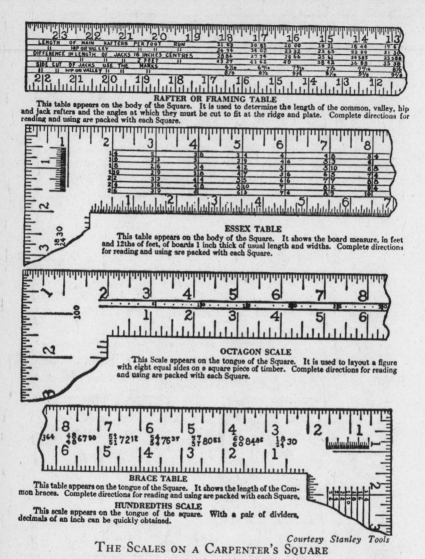

RAFTER OR FRAMING TABLE

This table appears on the body of the Square. It is used to determine the length of the common, valley, hip and jack rafters and the angles at which they must be cut to fit at the ridge and plate. Complete directions for reading and using are packed with each Square.

ESSEX TABLE

This table appears on the body of the Square. It shows the board measure, in feet and 12ths of feet, of boards 1 inch thick of usual length and widths. Complete directions for reading and using are packed with each Square.

OCTAGON SCALE

This Scale appears on the tongue of the Square. It is used to layout a figure with eight equal sides on a square piece of timber. Complete directions for reading and using are packed with each Square.

BRACE TABLE

This table appears on the tongue of the Square. It shows the length of the Common braces. Complete directions for reading and using are packed with each Square.

HUNDREDTHS SCALE

This scale appears on the tongue of the square. With a pair of dividers, decimals of an inch can be quickly obtained.

Courtesy Stanley Tools

THE SCALES ON A CARPENTER'S SQUARE

face of the work after it has been sawed, planed or chiseled.

Laying Out with a Square   Pencil versus Knife. A pencil is satisfactory for marking guide lines for roughing out woodwork. But because of the wide, relatively indefinite mark it produces, it cannot be used to lay out the accurate lines required in cabinet work and jointing. Such work should be laid out with the blade of a pocketknife or bench knife. The tip of the blade should be used. This makes a clean, accurate line for the meeting sides of joints.

Squaring Lines across a Board. When a board is to be cut off, planed or chiseled square, a guide line must be marked across its surface. The guide line must be exactly at the required point and must be square with the edges. Unless the board is wide enough to require a carpenter's square, a try square is used for the purpose. The stock of the try square is pressed firmly against the edge of the board with the left hand and the guide line marked along the blade with a pencil or knife blade.

To Square a Line around a Board. Either a carpenter's

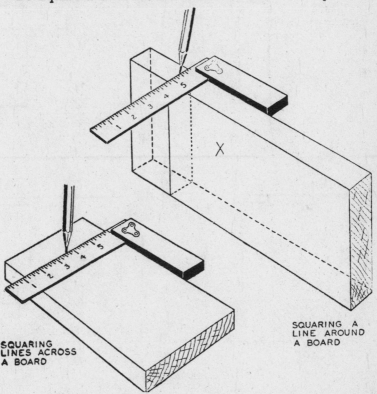

SQUARING A
LINE AROUND
A BOARD

SQUARING
LINES ACROSS
A BOARD

SQUARING

The beam or handle of the square should be pressed firmly against the edge of the board and a line marked along the blade. The longest part of a framing square is the blade but it is held against the edge of work under 14″ wide. The shortest part, the tongue, is held against the edge on work more than 14″ wide.

framing square or a try square may be used, depending upon
the width of the board. If the blade of the try square is not
long enough to reach all the way across the board, a carpenter's square should be used. Mark one edge and one face of
the board with an X so that they can be distinguished readily
as the working edge and the working face. Square a line
from the working edge across the working face by holding
the stock of the square firmly against the working edge and
marking a line along the blade. The working edge must be
perfectly flat so that the square will not rock. Lines are
squared from the working face across both edges. Then

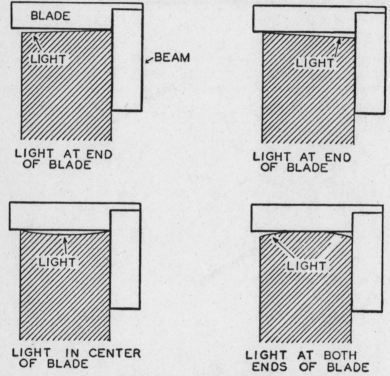

TESTING FOR SQUARENESS

Face the source of light so that light shines on the work. Place
the inside edge of the beam in full contact with one surface and slide
the square downward. Notice where the blade first comes in contact
with the surface. If the angle is not square, or if the surface is not
true, light will be seen between the blade and the work. If the angle
is square and the surface is true, all light will be excluded. The illustration shows tests indicating angles which are not square and surfaces which are not true.

holding the stock of the square against the working edge, square a line across the face on the side of the board opposite the working face.

Sliding T Bevel. This tool is a try square which can be adjusted to any angle. It is used for laying out angles other than right angles and for testing bevels. A bevel is any edge not at right angles to the face of a piece of wood. The hand tool used to produce a bevel is a plane. A sliding T bevel is used to lay out and test a bevel.

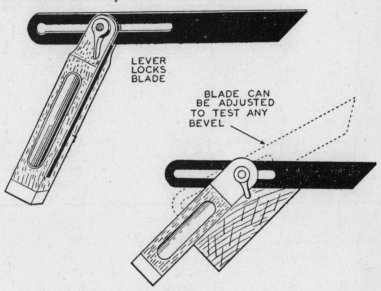

LEVER
LOCKS
BLADE

BLADE CAN
BE ADJUSTED
TO TEST ANY
BEVEL

THE SLIDING T BEVEL
FOR LAYING OUT AND TESTING BEVELS AND ANGLES

Gauging

Gauging is a term used by woodworkers to mean the marking of guide lines parallel to an edge, end or surface of a piece of wood. A good example of gauging is the marking of guide lines for chamfers.

Gauging with a Pencil. When a not too accurate guide line is to be drawn less than 1″ from an edge, a pencil and the fingers may be substituted for the tool called a marking gauge.

Suppose a guide line for a chamfer is to be gauged on a board 3/8″ from the edge. First, make a locating mark 3/8″ from the edge. Then grasp the pencil near its point with

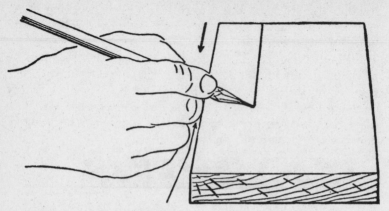

**THE THIRD FINGER
IS HELD AGAINST
EDGE OF WORK AND
ACTS AS THE HEAD
OF A MARKING GAUGE**

Gauging and Marking with a Pencil

Lines may be gauged or marked parallel to an edge at a distance of 1″ and less. Hold the pencil between the thumb and forefinger. The middle finger should rest against the edge. Place the pencil point on the work at the correct distance and slide the hand along.

the thumb and first and second fingers of the right hand and hold it at an angle of approximately 30 degrees to the surface to be marked. The third finger rests against the edge of the wood and acts as a guide in keeping the pencil mark parallel to the edge. The line may be gauged by pushing the pencil either away from the worker or toward him. In order to keep the line parallel to the edge, the angle of the pencil must be kept constant.

When accuracy is not an important consideration and a guide line is to be gauged more than 1″ from an edge, a pencil and a rule can be used. The point of the pencil is held against the end of the rule with the right hand. The rule is held between the thumb and forefinger of the left hand with the second finger against the edge of the wood as a guide. Both hands are moved in unison when the line is drawn.

The Marking Gauge. A marking gauge is used for gauging when accuracy is necessary. This tool, made of either wood or steel, consists of a beam about 8″ long on which a head slides. The head can be fastened at any point on the beam by means of a thumbscrew. The thumbscrew presses a brass shoe tightly against the beam and locks it firmly in position. When the gauge is used, a sharpened steel pin or spur cuts the gauge line on the wood. The spur is adjustable. It should project about 1/16″ and be filed so that it scores the wood like the point of a penknife blade.

A marking gauge must be adjusted by setting the head the proper distance from the spur. Although the bar of a marking gauge is graduated in inches, the spur may work loose or bend, thus calibrating inaccurately. Consequently, the careful workman pays no attention to the calibrations but

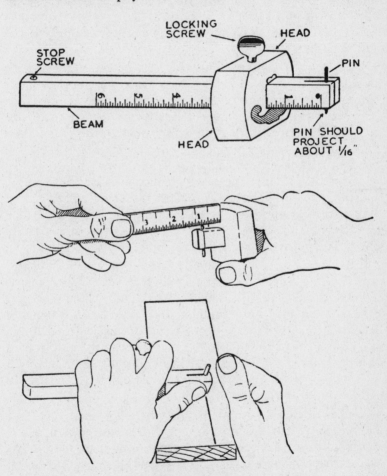

THE MARKING GAUGE
A tool for marking lines parallel to an edge or making marks at equal distances from an edge or end.

sets his gauge accurately by measuring between block and spur.

To draw a line after the gauge has been properly set, grasp the head with the palm and fingers of the right hand in much the same manner as you would a ball. Extend the thumb along the bar toward the pin. Press the head firmly against the edge of the piece to be marked and with a wrist motion tip it forward slightly until the spur just touches the wood. The line is made by pushing the gauge away from the worker while keeping the head firmly against the edge of the work at all times.

The spur must project no more than approximately 1/16" and must be kept sharp.

The Mortise Gauge. This tool is a marking gauge with two spurs. It is used chiefly for laying out mortises and tenons. The two spurs mark two parallel lines the distance between which can be changed by moving one of the spurs controlled by an adjusting screw in the end of the beam. The two spurs are set the proper distance apart first. Then the head is set the correct distance from them. The mortise gauge is then used in the same manner as a marking gauge.

Many mortise gauges are made with a single spur on the side of the bar opposite the one bearing the two spurs. This makes a dual purpose tool, for, turned over, the mortise gauge can be used as a marking gauge.

Levels. The level is a simple instrument which indicates a true vertical position or a true level position by means of a liquid sealed in a glass tube. The tube is mounted in a frame which may be aluminum, iron or wood. Aluminum levels, light in weight, will not warp or rust. Wood levels are light and are not cold to the touch when used outdoors in cold weather. Iron levels, which are heavier and which will rust, hold their shapes better and withstand more abuse than either wood or aluminum levels.

Levels are used chiefly in the construction and repair of buildings, and in the installation of machinery and workbenches. There are levels made especially for masons, levels for carpenters and levels for ironworkers and engineers. There is very little difference in any of these.

Carpenters and woodworkers generally use levels with either an aluminum or a wood frame, equipped with two, four or six glasses, as the tubes are called. One set of tubes is built in the frame at right angles to the other set. There is an air bubble in each tube. When a level is laid on a flat surface or held against a vertical surface, the surface is true level or true vertical, as the case may be, if the air bubble in one of the tubes is *in the center*. If the bubble is at either end of the tube or not exactly centered, the surface is not true level or not true vertical.

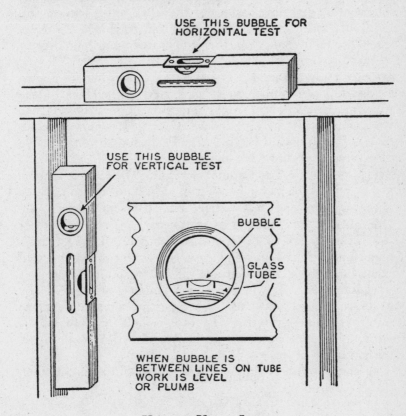

USE THIS BUBBLE FOR HORIZONTAL TEST

USE THIS BUBBLE FOR VERTICAL TEST

BUBBLE

GLASS TUBE

WHEN BUBBLE IS BETWEEN LINES ON TUBE WORK IS LEVEL OR PLUMB

How to Use a Level

8 Smoothing and Finishing

WHEN a job of woodworking has been completed, it is usually given a finish, meaning a protective and decorative coating of paint, lacquer, wax, stain, varnish, oil or shellac. The coating gives the surface of the work color, texture and durability and prevents the wood from warping or shrinking because of changes in the temperature and humidity of the atmosphere.

Before any finishing coat can be applied to woodwork to successfully accomplish these purposes, the surface of the work must be smooth. Final smoothing operations on fine woodwork are done by hand with scrapers and with sandpaper. Two types of scrapers for fine woodworking are the cabinet scraper and the hand scraper.

Scrapers and Scraping Operations

The Cabinet Scraper. The cabinet scraper has a beveled blade set in an iron frame with two handles. It resembles a spokeshave in appearance.

A cabinet scraper takes a much thinner shaving than a plane and it is used only on flat surfaces after they have been planed or on surfaces that are difficult to plane because of irregular grain. It will produce a smooth cut against the grain, making it indispensable for putting a smooth surface on cross-grained woods. The tool is held in both hands. Although it may be either pushed or pulled, it is probably pushed more often.

A sharp cabinet scraper takes off a thin even shaving,

THE CABINET SCRAPER
This tool takes a finer cut than a plane and is used for fine finishing and to remove marks left by a plane.

122

removing the slight ridges left by a plane. Dust instead of shavings indicates a dull blade. A scraper, no matter how sharp the blade is, will not work satisfactorily on soft wood. A scraper blade dulls quickly. If you watch an experienced scraper at work you will see him occasionally renew the edge of his blade by rubbing it with a burnishing tool. This can be done several times before the edge must be reground.

The blade used in a cabinet scraper has a beveled edge which has been turned slightly by drawing a burnisher along it (see page 125). The blade can be removed from the body of the scraper by loosening the adjusting and the clamp thumbscrews. A new blade is inserted from the bottom, between the body and the clamp with the bevel side toward the adjusting thumbscrew.

The blade is adjusted so that it is even with the bottom of the scraper body by placing the latter on a flat wood surface and pressing the blade down lightly against the wood. Then the clamp screws are tightened to hold it in this position. The adjusting screw is tightened until it just touches the blade and a trial cut is made. If one corner of the blade projects farther than the other, draw it back in by tapping the side of the blade near the top. If the blade does not project far enough to make a thin shaving, tighten the adjusting screw a little at a time between trial cuts until a fine shaving is produced.

The Hand Scraper. The hand scraper produces finer shavings than a cabinet scraper and can be used on both flat and curved surfaces. Veneers or veneered surfaces generally cannot be planed but must be scraped. A scraper is almost the only tool that will give satisfactory results in refinishing furniture. The common form of hand scraper is a rectangle of high-tempered hand saw sheet steel varying in width from 2″ to 3″ and in length from 4″ to 6″. Curved forms, called molding scrapers, are also made for scraping concave and convex curves in cabinetmaking, joinery and pattern work.

Some scrapers have square edges and others beveled edges. The edges of both are turned with a tool called a burnisher. A square-edge scraper makes a smoother surface but does not cut as fast as a scraper with a bevel edge. The square-edge produces a flatter surface but dulls sooner

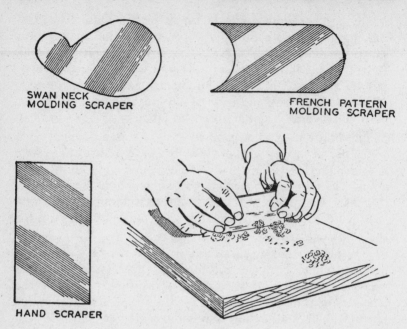

SWAN NECK
MOLDING SCRAPER

FRENCH PATTERN
MOLDING SCRAPER

HAND SCRAPER

HAND SCRAPERS

These steel blades remove finer shavings than the cabinet scraper and may be used for both flat and curved surfaces. Molding scrapers are made especially for curves of small radius.

than a bevel-edge. A square-edge scraper is used for finishing cabinet work and the faster cutting bevel-edge is used for floor scraping, and scraping the bright work (varnished woodwork) on boats prior to staining and varnishing.

How to Use a Hand Scraper. A hand scraper is grasped with the thumb and fingers of both hands. It may be either pushed or pulled as the grain of the wood requires. It produces a finer shaving when pulled than when pushed. If pulled, the top of the blade is tilted forward toward the operator. When pushed, the blade is slanted away from the operator. The angle between the blade and the work should be about 75 degrees. A chattering blade means it is held too straight. The blade will cut best when it is sprung to a slight curve by pressure of the thumbs. When a scraper becomes slightly dull, the edge can be renewed several times by rubbing with a burnishing tool. Finally it becomes so dull that it must be resharpened.

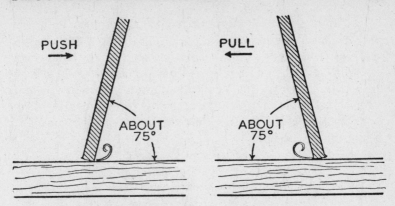

THE CUTTING ANGLE OF A HAND SCRAPER

The blade of a hand scraper must be held to the work at an angle of approximately 75°. The correct angle will depend upon how much turn is given the edge when it is sharpened and can be determined by feel. Use the angle at which the scraper cuts best.

Dressing Scraper Blades   A scraper does its work because the edge is turned to form what a mechanic calls a hook edge. It is not difficult to turn the

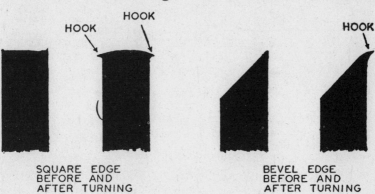

SQUARE EDGE BEFORE AND AFTER TURNING   BEVEL EDGE BEFORE AND AFTER TURNING

BURNISHER

SCRAPER EDGES

These magnified side views of both square-edge and bevel-edge blades show the turned edge or hook which does the cutting. A burnisher is used to turn the edges of a scraper.

edge but it is tricky enough to require experience. The best way to learn is to have a good mechanic show you the method. However, you can teach yourself by trial and error. Examine an edge with a magnifying glass after you have turned it. Then try it. You will soon learn how much hook is most desirable. If the edge is turned too far over it can be bent back slightly by drawing the point of the burnisher along under the burr.

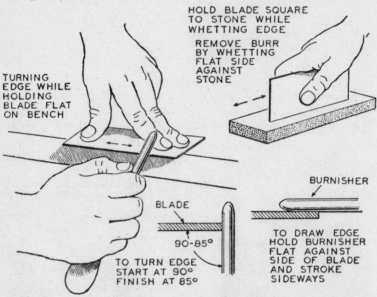

HOLD BLADE SQUARE TO STONE WHILE WHETTING EDGE

REMOVE BURR BY WHETTING FLAT SIDE AGAINST STONE

TURNING EDGE WHILE HOLDING BLADE FLAT ON BENCH

BURNISHER

BLADE

90-85°

TO TURN EDGE START AT 90° FINISH AT 85°

TO DRAW EDGE HOLD BURNISHER FLAT AGAINST SIDE OF BLADE AND STROKE SIDEWAYS

DRESSING A SQUARE-EDGE SCRAPER

Grind, file or whet to produce smooth square edge. Then draw and turn to form hook.

Sharpening Hand Scrapers for Square Edge Scraping. Some cabinet scrapers are supplied with plain edges which must be dressed before the scraper will cut. To dress a scraper:

1. Clamp the scraper in a vise and draw file the edges straight at right angles to the face of the scraper, using a smooth mill file. Round each corner very slightly. If the filing is properly done, it will produce perfectly square but rough edges which must be smoothed on an oilstone. The blade should not be hollow in the center.

2. Whet the edges of the scraper on an oilstone, holding the blade square to the surface of the stone. Do not

allow the blade to rock from side to side or it will produce a rounded edge. A square edge is necessary. A rounded edge on a scraper is useless.

3. Lay the scraper flat on the oilstone and rub to remove any burr which was produced by previously filing and whetting the edges. The edges should be very smooth, square and sharp.

4. Lay the scraper flat on the bench and draw the edge with three or four firm strokes of a burnisher held flat against the scraper. A cabinet burnisher is a piece of highly polished steel rod set in a hardwood handle. The burnisher is so hardened that without scratching itself it will turn the edge of a cabinet scraper and other edged tools. Some mechanics make their own burnishers from old 3-cornered files by grinding off the teeth and rounding the corners, leaving a smooth, round surface. A grinding wheel leaves too rough a surface which, therefore, must be smoothed to a polish by whetting it with a fine stone.

5. Clamp the scraper blade in a vise and turn the edge with a few strokes of the burnisher. Hold the handle of the burnisher in the right hand; hold the tip in the left and, after depositing a drop of oil on it, draw the burnisher toward you using a sliding stroke. Starting at the far corner

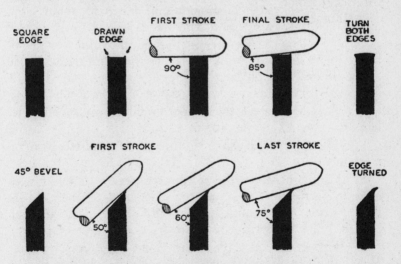

TURNING A SCRAPER BLADE TO FORM HOOK

A square-edge scraper is illustrated at top. The method of turning a bevel-edge scraper is illustrated below.

of the blade, draw the burnisher the full length of the blade. For the first stroke the burnisher should be held at 90 degrees to the face of the blade. Thereafter tilt the burnisher slightly and gradually until after five or six strokes it is at an angle of about 85 degrees. In this manner the edge is pressed out and turned slightly to form a hook.

Sharpening Bevel-edge Hand Scrapers. To dress a bevel-edge scraper:

1. File or grind the edge to a 30-degree bevel. If the former method is used, push the file forward and to one side with a sliding motion.

2. Whet the bevel side of the blade by the same method used to sharpen a chisel. Then, laying the face side of the scraper flat on the oilstone, rub it back and forth a few times to remove the wire edge.

3. Clamp the blade in a vise and run a burnisher along the keen edge to turn it. Make the first few strokes firm with the burnisher at an angle which is only a little greater than the bevel. Increase the angle until at the last stroke the burnisher is at an angle of about 75 degrees to the face of the blade. This produces a fast-cutting hook edge.

Resharpening the Bevel Edge of a Cabinet Scraper Blade

1. Clamp the blade in a vise with the cutting edge up. Remove the old burr with a smooth mill file held against the flat side of the blade.

2. Restore the old bevel by filing or grinding it to an angle of 45 degrees. If the blade is filed, use a smooth mill file pushing it sideways at the same time it is pushed forward. This will produce a smooth edge.

3. Whet the bevel to a smooth edge on an oilstone. Maintain the 45 degree angle.

4. Whet the blade, flat side down, on an oilstone to remove the wire edge.

5. Lay the blade on the workbench bevel side down with edge projecting slightly over the edge of the bench. Hold the burnisher flat against the flat side of the blade and rub it back and forth with a few firm strokes to draw the edge.

6. To turn the edge place the blade, edge up, in a vise. Rub a drop of oil on the burnisher. Make the first stroke firm with the burnisher at an angle 3 or 4 degrees greater than the bevel. Then make several firm strokes with the

burnisher at about 75 degrees to the face of the blade.

To Resharpen a Dressed Scraper. Oftentimes the cutting edge of a scraper blade can be renewed several times by a few strokes of the burnisher. After this it will be necessary to file and whet the edge. A square-edge blade must be filed square and whetted to a keen smooth edge and then have its edge turned with the burnishing tool. All vestiges of the hook edge must be filed or ground from the bevel-edge scraper, a new bevel formed and the edge turned in the manner already described.

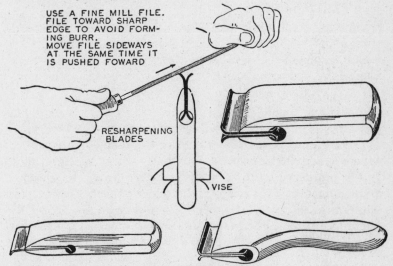

USE A FINE MILL FILE. FILE TOWARD SHARP EDGE TO AVOID FORMING BURR. MOVE FILE SIDEWAYS AT THE SAME TIME IT IS PUSHED FOWARD

RESHARPENING BLADES

VISE

WOOD SCRAPERS

These wooden-handled scrapers are useful to the amateur craftsman for floor scraping, scraping boats, removing old paint and varnish, etc. They are not satisfactory for fine work such as cabinet finishing. They can be resharpened with a mill file by using a draw filing stroke. The angle to which the cutting edge is ground at the factory should be maintained when resharpening. It is not necessary to turn the edge to form a hook. The curved shape of the blades gives somewhat the same cutting angle as a hook.

Sandpaper and Sanding

Not always with good reason, everyone seems to think he knows how to use sandpaper. The general opinion is that you rub it back and forth. Many are astonished to learn that there are many little tricks in its use.

Available in rolls and in sheets 9 x 11, sandpaper is made of tough paper which has been coated with glue and sprinkled with particles of quartz, garnet or flint. The variety known as garnet paper is red and is the best, not because of its color, but because it retains its sharpness longest. Sandpaper is graded according to the fineness of its grit. No. 3 is the coarsest and No. 8/0 is the finest. Nos. 1 1/2, 1, 1/2, 0 and 00 are the grades most commonly used. If the surface is rough and wavy it is either scraped or rubbed with No. 1 1/2 sandpaper. This grade leaves fairly large scratches. After it No. 1, No. 1/2 and finally No. 0 must be used. Each finer grade makes the scratches smaller until finally they become invisible.

Sanding. All work with planes, scrapers and other edge tools must be completed before sandpaper is used. When wood is rubbed with sandpaper, minute particles of grit become loosened from the paper and embedded in the wood surface. These quickly dull edge tools.

A surface should usually be sanded *with the grain*. Sanding across the grain tears and roughens the surface fibres and produces scratches which show through the finish. When sandpaper is rubbed over the wood at a slight angle to the grain instead of exactly with the grain, the abrasive will cut faster. This is especially true of soft woods such as white pine and of old lumber. Sanding at an angle cuts the fibers more easily. If the angle is not too great, a little rubbing with the grain will remove the scratches.

Unless a 9 x 11 inch sheet is folded, or divided, it is too large to use for hand sanding. The coarse grades can be folded more easily if the sheet is first flexed by grasping opposite edges and drawing the back over the edge of the workbench. A sheet is usually folded twice so that is is 4 1/2" x 5 1/2", or, if divided, it is torn into halves or quarters.

Sanding must be done carefully to avoid rounding edges and corners which are not supposed to be rounded. In many instances it is just as necessary to sand an edge or corner squarely as it is to plane it squarely. If the sandpaper is wrapped around a rectangular block of wood, rounding edges and some of the other pitfalls of sanding can be more easily avoided. A block of soft wood 4" to 5" long, 3" wide and 1" to 1 1/2" thick is a handy size. Much better than the block of wood is a block of cork of the same dimensions.

A piece of sandpaper 5 1/2" x 9", obtained by tearing a full-sized piece in half, can conveniently be wrapped around the block. It is held in place with the thumb and fingers. More even pressure can be applied with a block and a better surface produced.

Sandpaper soon fills up with fine wood particles. It will cut faster and longer if the dust is eliminated by slapping the sandpaper against a hard surface once in a while.

Concave surfaces are sanded with sandpaper wrapped around a piece of dowel or round stick.

Most convex surfaces can be sanded with a piece of sandpaper held in the hollow of the hand.

---

9   The Right Way to Use a Glass Cutter

THE skill and confidence with which a glazier cuts a pane of glass makes it look easy. It *is* an easy art, but the novice cannot expect to cut glass like a professional until he develops the right touch.

The Glass Cutting Tool. The ordinary steel wheel glass cutter is the tool of the glazier. It will give good service if properly used and cared for. On the other hand, it can be ruined quickly by mistreatment.

Close examination of the cutter will reveal that its work is done by a small sharp-edged wheel. This wheel is made of extremely hard steel and it revolves when it is drawn over a pane of glass. It must be kept sharp and free to turn easily. If it rusts, its sharp edge will be dulled and it may not turn. In that case throw the cutter away and buy a new one. The best way to prevent the wheel from rusting is to keep it wrapped in cotton or a small piece of rag saturated with sewing-machine oil.

Accurately speaking, the wheel-type glass cutter does not cut glass to size, it *splits* it. If the wheel is sharp and it is drawn over the glass at the right speed and pressure, it makes a fine score or groove by slightly crushing or pulverizing the glass under the edge of the wheel. The beveled

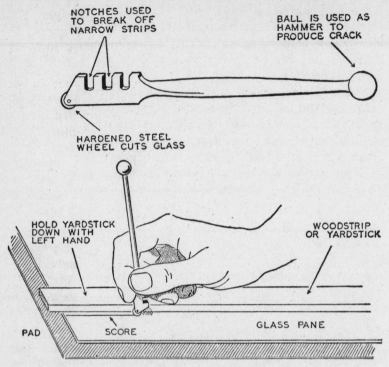

NOTCHES USED
TO BREAK OFF
NARROW STRIPS

BALL IS USED AS
HAMMER TO
PRODUCE CRACK

HARDENED STEEL
WHEEL CUTS GLASS

HOLD YARDSTICK
DOWN WITH
LEFT HAND

WOODSTRIP
OR YARDSTICK

PAD   SCORE   GLASS PANE

A GLASS CUTTER AND THE CORRECT WAY TO USE IT

sides of the wheel also act as wedges which push against the sides of the groove and pry the glass apart so that a crack is started.

Cutting Glass Panes Ordinary window glass comes in two thicknesses, single light and double light. Single light is the thinner and easier to cut. Plate glass up to 1/4" in thickness can be cut in the same manner as ordinary window glass. Safety glass, which consists of two or more glass sheets cemented together by a transparent plastic requires special cutting equipment.

Place Glass on Level Surface. Unless the pane which is to be cut is placed on a firm level surface, it may crack in an unexpected place. Place a piece of carpet or several layers of newspaper on a table and lay the glass on top. This pad between the table and the glass equalizes the pressure and greatly decreases the danger of breakage during the cutting operation. Make sure that the glass is thoroughly clean. Dirty glass does not cut well and also dulls the cutter wheel. Wet a small brush with turpentine and run it along the line to be cut. This not only makes the cutter work better, it also keeps it sharp longer.

To make a straight cut it is necessary to use a straight-edged guide strip to guide the cutter. A wooden strip is preferable because it does not slip as easily on a glass surface as metal. A wooden yardstick makes a good guide strip. The guide is held against the glass with the fingers of the left hand. The cutter is held in a vertical position in the right hand. The forefinger should be extended along the back of the cutter with the tip of the finger down near the wheel.

When placing the guide strip in position to cut a pane of glass to a specified size, bear in mind that the wheel does not cut exactly at the edge of the strip but makes the score or groove about 1/16" from it.

Start the score at the far end of the guide and draw the cutter toward you. Using the correct pressure in applying the wheel against the glass is one of the tricks of cutting glass. Too much pressure may crack the pane; too little may make an unsatisfactory score.

The Correct Pressure. The novice should practice on some old, *clean* pieces of window glass. Wipe a small brush, wet with turpentine, over the surface along the line to be cut. If the correct pressure is applied and the cutter is drawn toward you at the right speed, the wheel will make a scratching sound as it cuts the score mark into the glass. If the wheel is dull, or too much pressure is applied, the sound will be more like crunching than scratching.

Draw the cutter over the line *once* only. If it becomes necessary to doctor an imperfect score, do not use a new cutter for the purpose. Use an old one. Drawing a sharp cutter over a score mark the second time dulls it.

To cut a pane of glass it is necessary to make a continuous score mark all the way across from one edge to the other. If the score is properly made, a slight crack will be visible all the way along the score. The crack may not extend through from one surface to the other. It can best be seen from the side opposite the score. If the crack is continuous or nearly so, the glass will easily split into two pieces with little pressure. To part the glass along the score line, slide the pane over to the edge of the table so that the score line

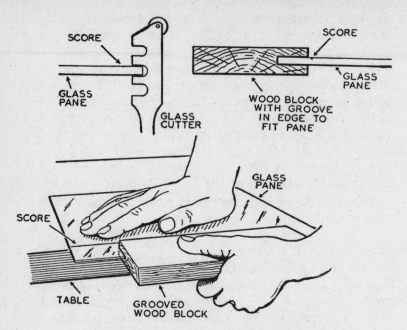

How to Break off a Narrow Strip
After the Score Has Been Cut

Slip a notch in the head of the cutter over the edge of a strip too narrow to grasp with the fingers. Use the notch which is the closest fit. A slotted wood strip is also useful for this purpose.

will be parallel to and projecting about 1/8″ beyond the edge. Hold the portion resting on the table firmly under the palm of the left hand. Grasp the projecting portion between the fingertips and palm of the right hand. Apply light firm pressure to break the pane into two pieces along the score line. The pane should lie on the table with the scored surface uppermost. The pressure which parts the glass is applied so as to open the crack which has been started by the cutter wheel. It can't be done the opposite way.

The novice may find it much easier to make a clean break along the score line by using a slotted wood strip. This device is especially useful when the piece to be broken off is narrow. A slot about 1/2″ deep is made in the edge of a wood strip about 3/4″ thick. The slotted strip should be nearly as long as the strip of glass which is to be broken off. The slot can be cut in the wood strip with a hand saw but a power driven circular saw will do the job much better.

Tapping. A pane of plate or double light glass will part along the scored line most easily and accurately if a continuous crack is started along the bottom of the groove. A sharp cutter and the right pressure will usually start this

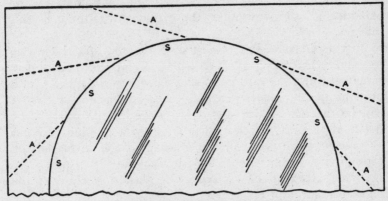

CUTTING GLASS TO PATTERN

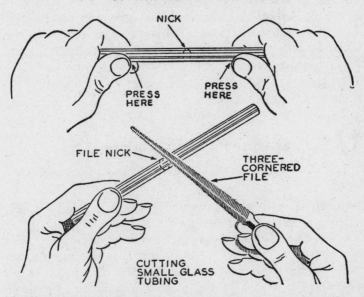

CUTTING SMALL GLASS TUBING

The line marked SSSSS in the upper sketch is a semi-circular score mark cut in a pane of glass. It is easier to crack the surplus glass away from a curved pattern if grooves are also scored with a glass cutter along several straight lines as indicated by the dotted lines marked A.

Small glass tubing can be cut to length by nicking it with a three-cornered file. It will then break easily at the nick.

crack when the groove is scored. If the crack does not appear then, it can generally be started by turning the pane over and tapping against the unscored surface with the end of the cutter handle. Tap directly over the line scored on the opposite side. A crack which is not continuous can be extended all the way along the groove by tapping in this manner.

Cutting Glass to Pattern. A simple method for the novice to employ in cutting glass to a pattern of specified dimensions is to first lay out a full-size drawing on paper. Use a drawing pen or a soft pencil to make the outline so that it will be distinct. Place this drawing under the pane to be trimmed to size. Circles, ovals and curved shapes are cut by tracing them through the glass with the cutter wheel. Straight lines are cut best by using a guide strip placed so that the cutter wheel will score the glass directly over the lines seen through the glass.

Cutting Glass Tubing. Glass tubing is cut by nicking it with a three-cornered file. Hold the tubing in both hands and apply pressure as if the glass were to be bent with the nick on the outside of the curve. It will crack apart at the nick. Glass rods may be cut in the same manner.

---

10 Sharpening Woodworking Tools

EXPERIENCED mechanics know the value of sharp tools. Tradition credits dull tools to the novice and less expert craftsman. A dull tool requires a lot more driving power than a sharp one; it does its work more slowly and less accurately. The time required to sharpen dull tools is regained many times in quality of workmanship and quicker operations.

All edged tools become dull with use and need to be resharpened. The proper sharpening of tools is one of the most important things for a mechanic to learn. To be in first class condition, edged tools such as chisels, gouges and planes should not only be ground to the correct angle but they should be honed until they are sharp enough to shave a hair off the back of your hand.

Files are used to sharpen saws and auger bits. Oilstones are used to renew the cutting edges of planes, chisels, scrapers, gouges and knives. After the latter have been resharpened several times it may be necessary to restore the original bevel of the cutting edge by grinding. A badly nicked edge must be ground also. To remove the wire edge which results from grinding it is necessary to whet the tool on an oilstone. The wire edge which is formed by grinding and also sometimes by whetting is a thin edge, so thin, in fact, that it bends back and forth like a piece of paper.

Oilstones   Tools are whetted on fine, hard stones called oilstones. There are two types, Washita oilstones, cut from a natural stone found in the Ozark Mountains in Arkansas and the artificial stones such as Carborundum and Aloxite. Carborundum is silicon carbide and Aloxite is aluminum oxide. Both substances are made in electric furnaces at Niagara Falls.

A few mechanics still use natural stones which have disadvantages. They cut slowly and only one kind of grit is available in one stone. To sharpen tools properly it is necessary to have a coarse grit stone for fast cutting and a fine grit stone for putting on a finishing edge. Combination artificial stones are obtainable having a coarse, fast cutting grit on one side and a fine, slower, smoother cutting grit on the other. A single combination artificial stone can therefore serve the purpose of two natural stones. Artificial stones cut faster than those that nature made.

Sharpening stones are called oilstones because when in use they are kept wet with oil. The pores of a dry stone become clogged with fine particles of steel sooner than the pores of a well-oiled stone. A clogged stone loses much of its cutting ability.

Never use water on a natural stone or a very fine grained artificial stone. Small particles of steel rapidly become imbedded in the surface of a stone wet with water. A black, shiny, glazed surface indicates this objectionable condition.

The oil used on an oilstone must be thin and it must not gum. Good oils for this purpose are Three-in-One and Pike

Oil. A mixture of equal parts of light machine oil and kerosene works well on most stones.

Carborundum stones may be used either dry, with oil or with water, but lubricated it will produce a cleaner, smoother edge.

Keep Sharpening Stones in Condition. To prevent an oil-stone from becoming gummy, keep it wrapped in a piece of cloth that is moistened with oil.

When a stone becomes gummy or clogged up it can be reconditioned by heating it in an oven. Place the stone in a shallow pan. Put two ten-penny finishing nails under the stone so that it is kept above the bottom of the pan thus avoiding contact with the oil and dirt which the heat will bring out. The oven should not be hot enough to evaporate the oil which oozes out. Wipe the stone dry while it is still hot.

When a stone has been worn hollow by long use, it is difficult to bring chisels and plane irons to a true straight edge. The stone needs dressing which is a simple task. A flat cast iron plate having a smooth surface at least three or four times the area of the surface of the oilstone is necessary. You will need about half an ounce of aluminum oxide powder of a grit size slightly coarser than that in the stone. Mix this with a little water until the consistency of the mixture is about that of thin mud. Smear this all over the surface of the plate and lay the worn sharpening stone on it face down. Use both hands, bear down with moderate pressure and scrub the stone around on the plate with a circular motion. It will not take long to grind the stone perfectly flat. Examine the surface being dressed and as soon as the hollow has disappeared, the job is done. You have a stone which is as good as new.

How to Sharpen Chisels Accurate work cannot be done with a dull chisel. It is very difficult to cut end grain on hard wood with a chisel which is even slightly dull. A chisel should always be kept sharp enough to shave the hair off the back of your hand.

Chisels are ground from time to time in order to restore the angle of the bevel. It is not usually necessary to grind the bevel each time the edge becomes dull. Grinding is essential when the cutting edge has become badly nicked and the nicks cannot be removed by whetting on a coarse oilstone, or when the bevel has become too short or rounded as a result of frequent whetting or of careless whetting.

A common oilstone of coarse grit on one side and a fine grit on the other is used to sharpen a chisel which does not require grinding. It is also used to whet a chisel after grinding.

The first "do not" in sharpening a chisel is *do not whet it on a dry stone*. Whetting tools on a dry stone will fill the

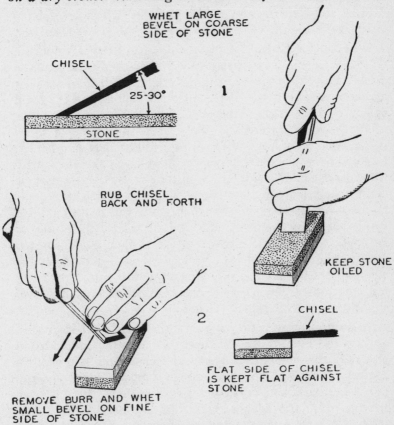

WHET LARGE
BEVEL ON COARSE
SIDE OF STONE

CHISEL

25-30°

1

STONE

RUB CHISEL
BACK AND FORTH

KEEP STONE
OILED

2

CHISEL

FLAT SIDE OF CHISEL
IS KEPT FLAT AGAINST
STONE

REMOVE BURR AND WHET
SMALL BEVEL ON FINE
SIDE OF STONE

SHARPENING A CHISEL

A chisel has a large bevel of 25 to 30 degrees which is whet on the coarse side of an oilstone (1) or ground on a wheel, and also a small bevel formed by whetting on the fine side of an oilstone. The small bevel and the flat side of the chisel form the cutting edge. The burr is removed by rubbing the flat side against the fine side of an oilstone (2). The final step in sharpening is to whet the edge on a piece of leather.

pores of the stone with fine particles of steel. The surface will become black and glazed; its whetting qualities will be spoiled.

The second "do not" is *do not use water or saliva*. Water will not prevent the stone from filling with steel particles. *Use kerosene and light machine oil.* The kind of oil used in the crankcase of an automobile is suitable if mixed with sufficient kerosene. Keep a bottle of oil handy on your bench and keep the oilstone covered with it when whetting tools. The oil will float the fine particles of steel which are ground off the tools and prevent them from clogging the stone.

Whetting a Chisel. The oilstone should be clamped in the bench vise or otherwise firmly held so that it cannot slide easily. Hold the chisel in the right hand with the bevel flat against the coarse side of the oilstone. Then raise the hand to lift the back edge of the bevel slightly off the stone. One of the important things to know when sharpening a chisel is that a chisel is like a plane iron in that it has *two bevels*. For ordinary work the large bevel which is ground with a wheel or the coarse side of an oilstone is usually at an angle of 25 to 30 degrees. For fine cutting and paring, the angle may be slightly less. The small bevel is the whetting bevel and is put on by the fine side of the oilstone. It is usually at an angle of 30 to 35 degrees. The proper angle for the whetting bevel is obtained by holding the chisel so that the whole of the large bevel is in contact with the flat surface of the stone, then raising the back edge of the ground bevel slightly off the oilstone.

It is only the whetting angle of the chisel that is ground against the face of the oilstone. Use the first and second fingers of the left hand to steady the chisel and hold it down against the face of the stone. With light pressure only, rub the chisel back and forth on the stone with smooth even strokes. Use the coarse side of the stone. After a few strokes, a burr or wire edge is produced. You can see the burr if you have good eyesight. You can see it plainly with a magnifying glass. It can also be felt by rubbing the finger tip against it *very lightly*. It is flexible enough to be bent back and forth.

This part of the sharpening process requires a little skill and experience. The main trick is to keep the hand steady, moving it back and forth *parallel* to the surface of the stone at all times. Do not rock the blade. The angle of the blade with the stone must remain constant during the whetting process. The entire surface of the stone should be used to avoid wearing a hollow in the center. The edge must be whet so that it is square with the sides of the chisel, not at a skew.

For whetting chisels and plane blades there is a very convenient gadget which holds them at a constant angle. This removes all the guesswork and gives the beginner a chance to do a whetting job equal to that of a skilled mechanic.

Removing the Burr. The burr, wire edge or feather edge (it is known by all three names) is removed by whetting it on the fine side of the oilstone or on a finer and harder separate stone. First, take a few strokes with the flat side of the chisel held *flat* on the stone. Be careful not to raise it even slightly. You must avoid putting the slightest bevel on the flat side, for then the chisel must be ground until the bevel is removed.

Next, turn the chisel over (bevel side down) and hold it at the same angle used when whetting on the coarse stone. Take two or three *light* strokes. These may be sufficient to remove the burr. On the other hand, it may be necessary to take one or two light strokes again with the flat side of the chisel flat against the surface of the stone in order to get rid of the burr.

Many mechanics give a finishing touch to the edge by stropping it a few times on leather or canvas. For this purpose a piece of leather cemented to a block of wood is a useful item in a tool kit.

Testing the Edge. Many craftsmen judge the sharpness of an edge by testing it on a thumbnail or by carefully feeling it with the ball of the thumb. If it is sharp, the edge will take hold on the nail; if not, it will slide. You can quickly learn to recognize a sharp edge by looking at it. A small magnifying glass or a watchmaker's glass will reveal whether or not the burr has been entirely removed and whether the edge is blunt or sharp. Your eye, unaided by a magnifier, will also tell you whether or not you have produced a really sharp edge by whetting. Hold the chisel where a good light will shine on the cutting edge. A keen edge does not reflect light. If there are no shiny or white spots, it is a good edge.

Grinding a Chisel. The amateur craftsman who uses his chisels only occasionally will seldom need to grind them. They can be kept sharp by whetting them on an oilstone or on a combination Carborundum stone. If, in the course of time, the edges and bevels do become worn down and need grinding, it is usually possible to have this done in some neighborhood shop. The grinding is done on a revolving stone. It is more difficult than whetting.

The grinding of chisels and other edged woodworking tools can be done on a variety of wheels, ranging from the old-fashioned foot-driven grindstone to the modern power-driven oil grinder. Grinding woodworking tools on a dry emery or Carborundum wheel requires care and experience. The tool must be dipped in water frequently to keep it cool. The hazard of using a dry grinder is the risk of burning the steel. The edge overheats; it turns a blue-black color, loses its temper and softens. Soft steel cannot be sharpened.

Burning must be avoided and can be by grinding very lightly, at the same time keeping kerosene or water dripping on the grinding wheel. An experienced mechanic can keep a tool cool during the grinding process by dipping it in water frequently. However, this is not as easy as it looks. It is difficult to repeatedly remove the tool from the wheel to cool it and then place it back against the wheel at the same angle each time.

An old-fashioned sandstone wheel, kept wet by water dripping on it, is really best for the novice at grinding woodworking tools, whether they are chisels, gouges, plane irons or spokeshave blades.

Modern plants where woodworking tools must be kept sharp are usually equipped with motor-driven oilstone grinders. The revolving wheel is in the form of a shallow cup. The outside edge is the grinding surface. Kerosene, fed through a tube from a small reservoir, drops on the inside of the cupped wheel and filters through to the surface. This grinder produces a smooth bevel with little danger of burning.

A small hand-driven grinder fitted with a Carborundum wheel of the right variety for woodworking tools can be used for plane iron, chisel, gouge and spokeshave grinding. The expert can turn the crank with one hand and hold the tool with the other. The beginner will find it much easier if he holds the tool with both hands while some one else turns the crank.

No matter which type of grinder is used, it should be one provided with an adjustable tool rest which can be set to produce the desired bevel. The face of the wheel should be smooth. If it is grooved or out of true it should be dressed or put into good shape with a Carborundum stick made for the purpose. The Carborundum stick, held against the revolving wheel, will cut the wheel.

Now let us return to chisel grinding. The wheel should turn toward the chisel. The bevel of the tool is held against the wheel lightly and moved from side to side evenly across its surface. The edge must be maintained at right angles to the sides of the chisel. A chisel which is off-square is said to be skewed and it is almost impossible to do accurate work with it. You can tell whether the chisel is against the wheel in such position to grind a bevel of the right angle by looking at it from the side when the wheel is not running. The chisel blade should rest on the tool rest in front of the wheel. When the right position has been found, grasp the chisel blade so that the back of the forefinger of the left hand touches the tool rest. The finger acts as a stop and you do not shift its position on the blade until you are through grinding. You can dip the tool in water from time to time or examine the bevel and always get the chisel back in the po-

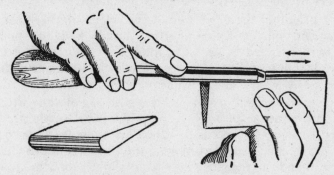

SHARPENING A GOUGE
The wire edge which remains after the bevel has been ground or whetted is removed by whetting with a slipstone.

sition on the wheel by using this finger as a guide. In grinding, the only motion of the chisel should be from side to side. If you move the chisel forward or back in relation to the wheel, you will change the bevel.

How to Sharpen a Gouge Sharpening a gouge is much the same as sharpening a plane iron or chisel. After all, a gouge is simply a chisel with a concave blade. There are two operations: grinding and whetting. Grinding is not always necessary. Generally, the edge may be whetted several times before it is necessary to grind it.

As already explained in Chapter 6 there are gouges with the bevel on the inside and those with their bevel on the outside.

An outside-bevel gouge is ground on an ordinary wet grindstone, a Carborundum wheel or an oilstone grinder. It is handled like a chisel. The tool rest on the grinder should be adjusted to suit the bevel required and the gouge moved across the edge of the wheel with a rolling motion during the grinding operation. The inside-bevel gouge is ground on a cone-shaped emery wheel.

The same precautions necessary for grinding chisels and plane irons are also taken for grinding gouges. Use light, firm pressure. Do not risk burning the edge by letting the tool become overheated. If a wet grinder is not available, dip the gouge in water frequently during the grinding process. Keep the bevel uniform, either flat or concave. A convex bevel produces an edge which will not cut well.

After grinding, the edge must be whetted. Rather than ordinary flat oilstones for whetting, small wedge-shaped stones with rounded edges to fit into concave surfaces are employed. These, called slipstones, should be kept wet with a mixture of kerosene and machine oil while being used.

A gouge is whetted just as a chisel is to remove the wire edge and produce a keen edge. First the bevel is whetted, then the flat side of the edge. When whetting the concave side of the gouge, instead of moving the tool over the stone, hold it still and rub the stone over it. A slight rotary motion should be given the gouge when it is being whetted.

While whetting the flat side of either type of gouge *use every care not to produce the slightest bevel on it.*

How to Sharpen Hand Saws The teeth of a hand saw do their cutting with their edges and points. Consequently these edges and points must be kept sharp for the saw to cut efficiently. Sharpening the teeth is done with a file. There are three operations: jointing and shaping, setting and filing.

The teeth of most saws are set alternately to the left and right so that the saw kerf or slot cut in the work is wider than the thickness of the saw blade. By thus reducing the friction between the saw and the work, it makes sawing easier. All saws need set. The teeth usually require setting if a saw has been used considerably before sharpening. However, it is not necessary to reset the teeth every time the saw is filed. In most instances a saw may be sharpened with a file four or five times before it needs setting. A hand saw should be treated like a knife or a chisel. As a knife or a chisel is whetted lightly every once in a while to keep its edge keen, so from time to time the teeth of a saw should be touched up with a file. If this is done, the saw will cut longer and better; its set will remain longer.

When a Hand Saw Needs Filing and Setting. A mechanic can tell when a saw is dull or when it needs setting by its feel when he cuts wood with it. He can also tell by examining the teeth. If the teeth are uneven, if the points and edges are not sharp or if there is not enough set, he can see it. The edges and points are easier to see when they are dull. They reflect more light. Sharp edges and points are almost invisible.

Study the teeth of a new saw or one which has just been sharpened by an expert. Then look carefully at the edge of a saw which has had a great deal of use without being sharpened. Feel the points of the teeth on a sharp saw and a dull saw. You can readily see and feel the difference.

Who Can Sharpen a Saw. Many fairly skillful woodworkers cannot sharpen a hand saw properly except with a saw-filing machine. The reason is that they cannot use a file well. If you can file accurately, you can file a saw after a little practice. It is advisable for the beginner to practice on an old saw with a new one before him as a guide.

The filing stroke must be kept level. Efficient saw filing demands a steady hand. If you cannot do a good job of hand filing, let someone who knows how sharpen your saws for you or else use a filing guide and clamp. This device is especially designed for those not experienced in filing hand saws. It holds the file at the proper angle and guides it. The operator merely pushes the file back and forth and moves it from tooth to tooth.

The Equipment Necessary. To file the teeth of most saws properly, the blade must be held rigidly in a vise. The best equipment for this purpose is a saw vise. This is an inexpensive device which can be purchased at hardware stores. The best substitute, when a saw vise is lacking, is a large machinist's vise and two smooth pieces of hardwood approximately 12" x 2" x 3/4". The saw blade is placed between the wood strips and clamped in the vise. The handle of the saw should be to the right and the toothed edge should not project far above the wood strips. The strips should be parallel to the toothed edge of the saw. The saw teeth must be held firmly so that they do not vibrate when filed. Those directly over the vise jaws are held most firmly. The saw can be shifted from time to time as the filing proceeds.

When a saw vise is used, the blade is placed between the jaws with the handle to the right. The toothed edge should not project far above the jaws and should be parallel to them.

If the teeth of a saw are uneven, irregular in size or shape or incorrectly shaped due to misuse of the saw or improper sharpening, it is useless to file and set the saw without first performing the operation called jointing. This is done with a tool called a hand saw jointer or with an 8" or 10" mill bastard file and will be explained in detail in a later paragraph. The file used for saw sharpening must be the right one for the job. It must be of the correct design, cut and size for the kind of saw and the kind of teeth to be filed. Saws are of many types and the files required for saw sharpening must necessarily be of considerable variety.

The files used for sharpening the teeth of a hand saw have a triangular section. They are single cut files, are made in lengths from 3" to 12" and are called slim taper files.

The proper size of file to use for any particular saw is determined by the point of the saw, or, in plainer words, the number of tooth *points* to the inch of length. This number is usually stamped on the blade near the handle. If it is not stamped on the blade, count the number of tooth points to the inch, measuring one inch from the point of any tooth including both the first and last points. When counting the tooth points on a rip saw, bear in mind that the teeth at the point of the blade are closer together than elsewhere on the blade. To determine the point of a rip saw, count the tooth *points* per inch at the *center* or *butt* of the blade. If seven points are counted, the saw is said to be a "seven point" saw. Five points indicate a "five point" saw, etc. (See page 50 for illustration.)

When you know the point of the saw to be sharpened, select the proper file by using the following table as your guide.

> For 4 1/2, 5, 6 point saws use a 7″ slim taper file
> For 7, 8 point saws use a 6″ slim taper or a 7″ extra slim taper file
> For 9, 10 point saws use a 5″ slim taper file
> For 11, 12, 13, 14, 15 point saws use a 4″ to 4 1/2″ slim taper file
> For 16 point saws and finer use a 4 1/2″ to 5″ No. 2 cut slim taper file

The First Step. Setting, when it is required, must be done *before* the filing is begun. Before the teeth are set, the first step is to inspect them carefully and make sure their points are even. This is the operation already mentioned called jointing and can be done with a saw jointer or with an 8″ or 10″ mill bastard file. When a file is to be used for jointing, a special holder can be obtained but is not necessary.

The saw jointer opens and closes like a hinge so that it can be slipped over the toothed edge of the saw blade and run back and forth over the teeth. It is fitted with a file. The jointer eliminates any chance of tipping the file so that the points of the teeth are rounded at the sides. Anyone can use a jointer. Skill is required to use a file for jointing.

If a mill file is used, place the saw in the vise and lay the file lengthwise on the teeth. Pass the file lightly lengthwise along the tops of the teeth the full length of the blade until the file touches the top of every tooth. Careful examination of the teeth will show that some have been flattened on top while others were barely touched.

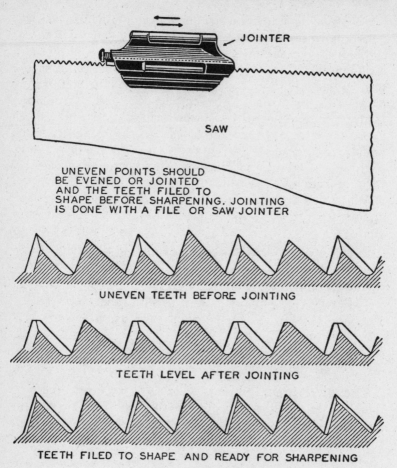

UNEVEN POINTS SHOULD
BE EVENED OR JOINTED
AND THE TEETH FILED TO
SHAPE BEFORE SHARPENING. JOINTING
IS DONE WITH A FILE OR SAW JOINTER

UNEVEN TEETH BEFORE JOINTING

TEETH LEVEL AFTER JOINTING

TEETH FILED TO SHAPE AND READY FOR SHARPENING

JOINTING SAW TEETH

Jointing evens the teeth prior to setting and filing. It is not necessary unless the points of the teeth are uneven.

Before the saw can be sharpened each one of the flattened teeth must be restored to its original size and shape by filing. To be done properly, this operation requires considerable skill. The novice should practice on an old saw with a new one before him as a model. Clamp the saw in the vise with the handle to the right and use the same file which will be used later in beveling the teeth. A 6″ slim taper file is suitable for the average handsaw. Filing should be begun in the gullet nearest the handle. Hold the file at right angles to the blade and file straight across. Do not bevel the teeth when filing them to shape. Continue until all teeth have been filed to shape.

If the teeth are very uneven, do not attempt to make them all the same height in one jointing. Joint only the highest teeth and file these flattened teeth into shape before proceeding (see **Filing the Hand Crosscut Saw and Filing the Hand Rip Saw.**) Then joint the teeth a second time. This time the file can be passed over the teeth until it touches them all.

Remember to hold the file flat when jointing. Do not allow the file to tip or rock from one side to the other. Remember also that if you joint the teeth more than necessary, you are making extra work for yourself in filing them back to shape.

Setting the Teeth. A hand saw does not need jointing every time the teeth are sharpened. And as already mentioned, the teeth of a first grade hand saw do not need setting every time that they require a light sharpening. In general, a well-tempered hand saw may be lightly filed four or five times before it requires setting. It is always necessary to set the teeth after they have been jointed and shaped.

The only satisfactory way to set saw teeth is to use the tool made expressly for the purpose—the sawset. There are

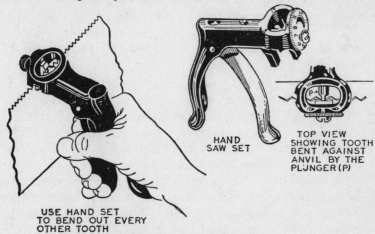

HAND
SAW SET

TOP VIEW
SHOWING TOOTH
BENT AGAINST
ANVIL BY THE
PLUNGER (P)

USE HAND SET
TO BEND OUT EVERY
OTHER TOOTH

PISTOL GRIP HAND SAWSET

Squeezing the handle moves a plunger which bends one tooth at a time. A graduated plate gives the correct anvil setting for 5- to 11-point saws. The right-hand sketch shows a saw tooth in position between anvil and plunger.

two types of sawsets made for the average user. One type resembles a pair of pliers and is operated by squeezing the handles together. Squeezing the handles moves a plunger working against a cylindrical drum of uneven thickness. The edge of the drum is marked to show the proper adjustment. The numbers correspond with the numbers indicating the points to the inch. The bench type of sawset attaches to the workbench or table and can be operated by striking the plunger with a mallet or working the plunger by foot power. Both types accomplish the same result—they bend the teeth slightly so that the width of the cut made by the saw will be greater than the thickness of the blade.

A sawset must be adjusted to suit the point or number of teeth per inch on the saw to be set. No matter whether the teeth are coarse or fine, the alternate teeth are set in opposite directions on both a cross-cut and a rip saw to a distance of about *half the thickness of the teeth* and the set *should not go lower than half the tooth*. If too much of a tooth is bent it may crack or break off.

Set the teeth in the same direction in which they were previously bent.

When the hand type of sawset is used, the saw should be clamped in a vise. The teeth which were originally bent away from the worker, that is, every other tooth, are all set first. The saw is then reversed in the vise and the remaining teeth are set in the same way, namely, away from the worker.

Soft woods and wet woods are cut most easily with a saw which has coarser teeth and more set than the saw which is preferable for dry, hard woods. A saw with a great deal of set does not leave a surface which is as smooth as that produced by a saw with fine teeth and not so much set. The latter is best for fine work on dry, hard woods.

The blade of a taper-ground saw tapers in thickness from the toothed edge to the back edge. It also tapers slightly from butt to point along the back. The taper provides part of the clearance necessary for easy running and consequently the teeth require very little set.

In setting a saw blade, it is essential to give every tooth the same amount of bend. The toothed edge must be the same width from point to butt and the teeth must project the same distance on both sides of the blade. Otherwise the saw will run out of line and fail to cut true.

Filing the Hand Cross-cut Saw. This saw should be clamped in the vise with the *handle to the right*. Since the filing is begun at the point of the saw and progresses toward the handle, the point should be clamped in the jaw when starting. As the filing progresses the saw is moved toward the left in the vise.

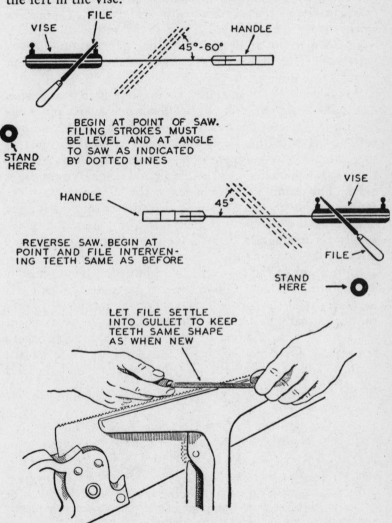

FILING THE HAND CROSS-CUT SAW

The V-shaped space between two teeth is called the gullet. The saw should be placed in the vise so that the bottoms of the gullets of the teeth are 1/8″ above the jaws of the vise or the wood strips used in the vise. If the blade is any higher than this, it will vibrate and chatter when filed. Chattering quickly dulls the file. A very keen edge cannot be produced on a chattering saw.

On this page is an enlarged sketch of the teeth on a hand cross-cut saw as they were when new and as they should be when you have filed them back to shape and a keen cutting edge. Notice the angles. On another page is an enlarged sketch of the teeth on a hand rip saw as they are when new. Observe the differences.

Stand in front and slightly to the left of the saw vise. Select the *first tooth that is set toward you* and place the file in the gullet to the *left* of this tooth. Hold the file perfectly level with the file handle swung toward the left so that the file is at an angle of approximately 60 degrees to the blade. The handle of the file should be held in the right hand. The thumb and forefinger of the left hand grasp the tip of the file to steady it. At the correct angle with the blade, the file should rest firmly in the gullet and touch evenly on the bevels of two teeth. It should cut on the push stroke only and file the back of the tooth to the left and the front of the tooth to the right at the same time. It will help the beginner to find the correct angle for the file if he places it in the gullet between two of the unused teeth that can usually be found at the handle end or butt end of the saw. Let the file find its own bearing against the teeth it touches. Observe the shape and bevel of these unused teeth and the angle of the file. Try to reproduce these at the point of the saw.

THE BEVEL IS IMPORTANT

Too much bevel causes the point of the teeth to score too deeply and the kerf to clog. Teeth beveled to a long front as at A and B are best suited to soft woods. A shorter bevel, as shown at C and D, is best for medium-hard woods.

The file must be kept level throughout the file stroke. Be sure the file sets down well in the gullet, finds its own bearing against the teeth and is not allowed to tip upward or downward during the forward cutting stroke. If jointing the teeth has left flat tops, at this time such teeth should be filed only until *one-half* the flat top is cut away. Lift the file from the gullet and, skipping the next gullet to the right, place the file at the same angle in the second gullet toward the right. Follow the same procedure until every other gullet has been filed and you reach the handle-end of the saw. Be careful to keep the file level and always file at the same angle.

Now reverse the saw in the vise so that the handle is to the left. The point of the saw should be in the vise jaws and the bottoms of the gullets should be 1/8" above the jaws of the vise as before. Stand in front and slightly to the right of the vise. Beginning again at the point of the saw, place the file in the gullet to the *right* of the first tooth set *toward* you. This is the first gullet skipped when you were filing the other side of the saw. Hold the file level and swing the handle to the *right* to form the desired angle to the right instead of to the left as when the first side was filed. File every other gullet all the way to the handle. File until the remaining half of the flat tops have been cut away and the teeth are sharpened to a point.

Sharpening Mitre Saws, Back Saws and Dovetail Saws. These are crosscut saws and are therefore filed as such. Because of their fine teeth, they are filed with 4 1/2" extra-slim taper file.

Filing Hand Rip Saws. The teeth of a hand rip saw are set and jointed in the same manner as those of a hand crosscut saw. Follow the same procedure. Select the same file that you would use if the saw were a crosscut having the same number of teeth per inch.

Place the saw in the vise with the handle to the right and the bottom of the gullets about 1/8" above the vise jaws. Notice from the illustration or from the saw itself that the teeth of a rip saw are so shaped that they act like a row of miniature chisels, one following along after the other. The teeth are filed so that the tooth *points*, not the tooth edges, do the cutting. *Rip* saws are filed with the file level and

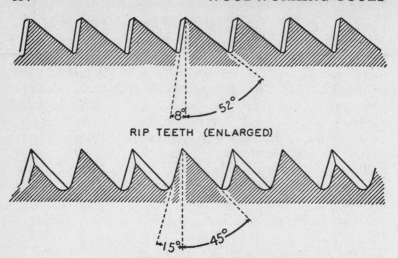

RIP TEETH (ENLARGED)

CROSS CUT TEETH (ENLARGED)

RIP AND CROSS-CUT TEETH

The rip saw tooth has an angle of 8 degrees on the front and 52 degrees on the back. The front of the cross-cut saw tooth should have an angle of 15 degrees and the back of the tooth an angle of 45 degrees.

straight across the saw at right angles to the blade. Also notice from the illustration that the angle on the front of each tooth is 8 degrees and not 15 degrees as in the case of a crosscut saw, and that the angle at the back is 52 degrees and not 45 degrees. The file should be so held as to maintain these angles. Place the file in the gullet to the left of the first tooth set toward you and start filing. Continue to file in every second gullet so as to bring every other tooth to a square edge. Then reverse the saw in the vise end for end so that the handle is at the left. Start filing at the point again. Place the file in the first gullet skipped when filing from the other side. Continue to file in every second gullet until the remaining teeth have been brought to a square edge.

The Shape and Angle of the Saw Teeth Are Most Important. Filing a hand saw properly is more of an art than the procedure described in the past few pages would indicate. The skilled saw filer pays a great deal of attention to the angle of the teeth and also to the bevel of the teeth on a cross-cut saw.

Angles of 15 degrees at the front and 45 degrees at the

back for cross-cut saws and 8 degrees at the front and 52 degrees at the back for rip saws are the most satisfactory for general use. If the front angle is made smaller, the teeth will have too much hook or pitch. This causes the saw to grab in the slot and the sudden stop may bend the blade.

Experience is the best guide to the amount of bevel on the front and back of a cross-cut saw. The illustration on page 152 should be helpful to the beginner. Two different teeth are illustrated. Notice that both have the same amount of bevel at the front edge. Teeth like that shown at A with the same amount of bevel front and back have a long bevel at the point (as shown in the end view at B) which best suits them to soft woods where rapid cutting rather than fine work is desirable. Teeth like that shown at C with less bevel on the back than at the front have a shorter bevel on the point (as shown in the end view at D) which best suits them to medium hard woods.

Filing a Cross-cut Saw. The common type of cross-cut saw used for hand sawing large timbers and logs has two sets of teeth, called cutters and rakers. The cutters, slightly longer than the rakers, do the cutting. The rakers clear out the cut. There are usually more cutter teeth than raker teeth.

The points of the teeth should be jointed if they are not of uniform height. The tops of raker teeth should be from 1/100″ to 1/64″ below the tops of the cutter teeth.

A mill file or a special cross-cut saw file is used to file all cutting teeth to a sharp point. If the saw blade is clamped in a saw vise tilted away from the filer at an angle of about 45 degrees, it will be easier to file the cutter teeth than if the blade is in a vertical position.

The raker teeth are best sharpened with the blade in a vertical position. They are filed straight across with a mill

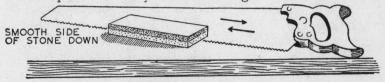

SMOOTH SIDE
OF STONE DOWN

DRESSING THE TEETH

After filing and before setting, lay the saw flat on a bench or table and rub a fine oilstone lightly over the teeth to remove any burr or wire edge. Dress both sides of the saw in this way.

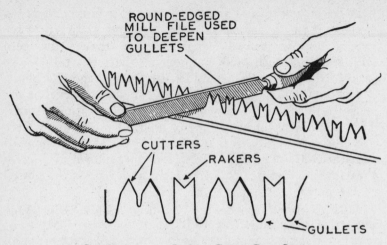

ROUND-EDGED
MILL FILE USED
TO DEEPEN
GULLETS

CUTTERS

RAKERS

GULLETS

SHARPENING A LARGE CROSS-CUT SAW

The teeth should be sharpened by filing with a mill file or a special cross-cut saw file. A round-edged mill file is used to deepen the gullets when necessary.

file or a special cross-cut saw file. A cant saw file may be used to finish both sides of the raker teeth at the same time.

If the saw has been sharpened so many times that the teeth have been shortened making the gullets too shallow, deepen them with a round edge file.

A "Don't" for the Beginner. Don't be lazy and try to save time and trouble by filing all teeth from the same side of the blade. Never do this. It will cause the saw to run to one side.

How to Sharpen Plane Irons Sharpening a plane iron is like sharpening a chisel. There are two operations: grinding and whetting. Grinding is not always necessary. Ordinarily the edge may be whetted several times before it is necessary to grind it. When the cutting edge of a plane iron has been nicked or been whetted on an oilstone so often that its bevel has become short, it must be ground on an emery wheel or grindstone.

The first thing to do after the plane iron has been removed from the plane (if it is a double plane iron) is to separate the iron from the cap. This is done by loosening the screw and sliding it along to the end of the slot where the head will pass through the hole. You cannot sharpen a double plane iron with the plane iron cap in place. An ex-

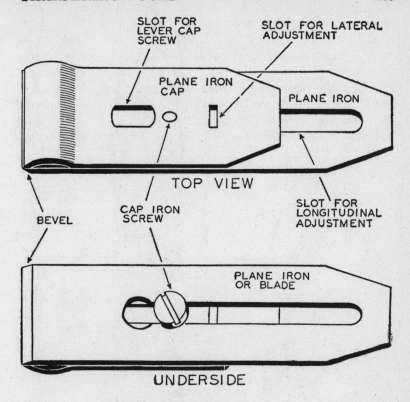

THE DOUBLE PLANE IRON

amination of the plane iron will reveal whether or not it needs grinding prior to whetting.

Grinding a Plane Iron. A plane iron is more difficult to grind than a chisel or a gouge. The hazards which confront the novice in grinding a plane iron are: burning the edge and the difficulty of forming the correct bevel at *90 degrees to the sides of the iron.*

Grinding wheels for wood-working tools have already been discussed in the section on grinding a chisel. Read this carefully before attempting to grind a plane iron. No matter which type of grinder is used, it should be one which is provided with an adjustable tool rest. The wheel should turn toward the tool. The edge must be dressed smooth.

The right bevel or grinding angle is 25 to 30 degrees. To get this angle, the length of the bevel ground should be equal to fully twice the thickness of the tool. The wheel should turn toward the tool and the latter should be moved from side to side across the edge of the wheel. Only a light pressure against the wheel is used. Too much pressure causes overheating, spoiling the tool. The edge should be straight and at right angles to the sides of the plane iron. Test it for squareness with a small try square. If out of square, it can be corrected by rubbing the cutting edge on the edge of a medium fine oilstone. The edge of the stone is used because,

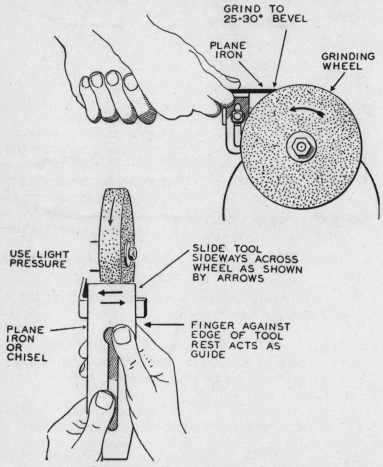

GRIND TO
25-30° BEVEL

PLANE
IRON

GRINDING
WHEEL

USE LIGHT
PRESSURE

SLIDE TOOL
SIDEWAYS ACROSS
WHEEL AS SHOWN
BY ARROWS

PLANE
IRON
OR
CHISEL

FINGER AGAINST
EDGE OF TOOL
REST ACTS AS
GUIDE

GRINDING A PLANE IRON OR CHISEL

Both hands are needed to hold the tool. When a hand-driven wheel is used, a second person must turn the crank. Dip the tool in water frequently to cool and keep edge from burning. The lower sketch shows the position of the tool and of the hands when looking down on them.

unless the stone is new, the flat surfaces are seldom true.

Avoid forming a bevel which is much outside the 25 to 30 degree angle recommended. A short thick bevel of more than 30 degrees will not enter the wood easily. A long thin bevel of less than 25 degrees is weak enough to nick easily.

If you have a protractor, you can measure the bevel in degrees and grind it to the desired angle. A bevel of 25 degrees makes the plane slightly easier to push than one of 30 degrees. The 30 degree angle is best for hard wood full of knots. The finished bevel should be flat or slightly concave. A rounded or convex bevel produces an edge which cuts poorly.

The plane iron is ground until a fine burr or wire edge appears.

Whetting a Plane Iron. After grinding, a plane iron is whetted on an oilstone to produce the final keen cutting edge.

The oilstone should be clamped in a vise so that it can-

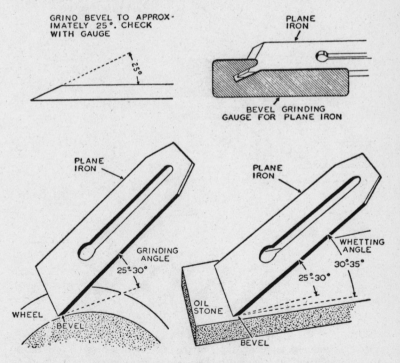

THE CORRECT GRINDING AND WHETTING ANGLES

not move. The whetting process is begun by holding the plane iron, bevel side down, on the flat surface of the oilstone. Hold the plane iron in the right hand. Use two or three fingers of the left hand to help hold the iron against the stone. At first the whole bevel should be in contact with

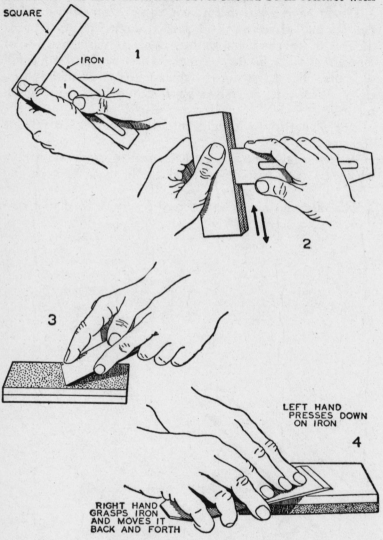

WHETTING A PLANE IRON

1. Testing the edge of a plane iron for squareness. 2. Squaring an edge by rubbing it against the side of an oilstone. 3. Whetting the bevel side. 4. Whetting the flat side to remove a wire edge.

the stone. Then the back edge is raised very slightly and the plane iron moved back and forth over the stone.

The whetting bevel is at a slightly greater angle than the grinding bevel, usually 30 to 35 degrees. The bevel must be kept straight. Rocking the iron even slightly as it is moved back and forth produces a rounded bevel which will not cut efficiently. Hold the iron firmly, keep an even moderate pressure against the stone, and move the hands parallel to the stone. Keep the surface of the stone moist with oil. Move the iron sideways slightly over the surface of the stone as well as to and fro to wear the stone evenly, making certain that all parts of the cutting edge come into contact with the stone. The main pressure should be on the forward stroke and the angle between the iron and the stone *must be kept constant.* Usually from six to a dozen strokes will be enough.

The plane iron is then reversed and its flat side placed in contact with the oilstone. Rubbing it back and forth a few times will remove the wire or feather edge. Keep both

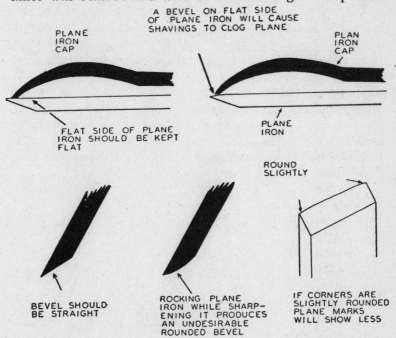

TIPS ON WHETTING A PLANE IRON

hands on top of the cutter so as to avoid any possibility of lifting it, thereby producing a bevel on the flat side of the iron. If this should happen, the cap iron will not fit tightly, causing shavings to clog the plane. If the slightest bevel is produced on the flat side, the plane iron must be reground.

If the wire edge is not removed after a few strokes with the *flat* side of the plane iron held *flat* on the stone, reverse the iron and whet the bevel side again. Usually the feather edge drops off quickly and is found on the oilstone in the form of a silvery thread.

The whetting is finished by drawing the edge over a smooth wood block or a leather strop. A sharp plane edge is invisible. If it is dull, the edge will appear as a fine white line. If the shiny edge of bluntness or a nick can be seen, repeat both whetting processes.

The thumbnail test can be applied to plane irons as well as chisels. If the edge is allowed to rest on the thumbnail by its own weight and it takes hold in the nail, it is sharp. If it slides over the nail, it is not sharp.

Plane marks will show less on a surface which has been planed if the corners of the cutting edge are very slightly rounded. For this reason the cutting edge of the plane iron in a jack plane is often given a slight curve during the whetting operation.

How to Assemble a Double Plane Iron. A newly sharpened plane iron must be handled with care to avoid nicking its keen edge. To put a plane iron and the plane iron cap together, lay the plane iron cap across the flat side of the plane iron with the screw in the slot. Then pull it down and away

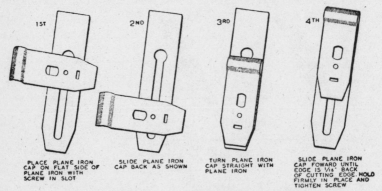

1ST   2ND   3RD   4TH

PLACE PLANE IRON CAP ON FLAT SIDE OF PLANE IRON WITH SCREW IN SLOT   SLIDE PLANE IRON CAP BACK AS SHOWN   TURN PLANE IRON CAP STRAIGHT WITH PLANE IRON   SLIDE PLANE IRON CAP FOWARD UNTIL EDGE IS 1/16" BACK OF CUTTING EDGE. **HOLD** FIRMLY IN PLACE AND TIGHTEN SCREW

How to Assemble a Double Plane Iron

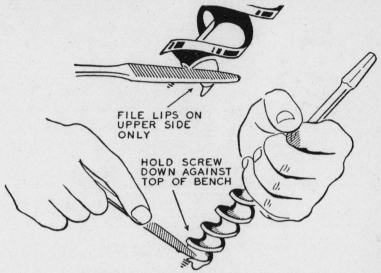

FILE LIPS ON
UPPER SIDE
ONLY

HOLD SCREW
DOWN AGAINST
TOP OF BENCH

FILING THE LIPS OF AN AUGER BIT

from the cutting edge. When it is almost to the end of the
slot turn the cap parallel to the iron. Holding cap and iron
together, slide the cap forward toward the cutting edge of
the iron until the edge of the cap is just back of the cutting
edge. The cap must not be moved or dragged across the
cutting edge for it will nick and dull it. For general work
the edge of the plane iron cap should be about 1/16" back
of the cutting edge. It should be set as near to the cutting
edge as possible when the plane is to be used on cross grain
and curly wood. When the cap is in its proper position hold
the cap and iron firmly together and tighten the screw which
holds the two parts together.

How to Sharpen an Auger Bit
An auger bit becomes dull if it is frequently used to bore holes in hard wood.
In repair work, an auger cutting its way
into old woodwork sometimes encounters a nail or screw
which bruises the cutting edges. It can be resharpened by filing with a specially designed auger bit file. These files are
small, double-ended and tapered so that the narrow portion
can be used on small diameter bits and the wider portion on
larger bits. One end of the file is made with its sides safe
or uncut while the other end has cut edges. In sharpening a
bit both the lips and the nibs or spurs are filed. The safe
portions of an auger bit file make it easy to file either the

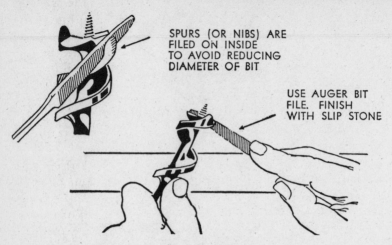

SPURS (OR NIBS) ARE
FILED ON INSIDE
TO AVOID REDUCING
DIAMETER OF BIT

USE AUGER BIT
FILE. FINISH
WITH SLIP STONE

FILING THE NIBS OF AN AUGER BIT

lips or nibs without damaging adjacent surfaces.

When filed, the bit may be held in a vise or firmly held down against the top of the workbench. The lips should be filed on the top surface of the cutting edge. Remove sufficient metal to take any bruises out of the edge. Remove an equal amount from both lips. Follow the original bevel. The lips are filed on the *top surface only* to maintain the clearance on the under side.

The nibs or spurs are filed on the *inside only* in order to maintain the diameter of the bit. For an extra keen edge on both lips and nibs, after filing, whet with a slipstone.

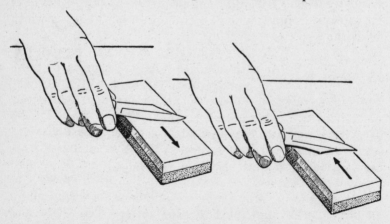

SHARPENING A KNIFE BLADE

11   Directions for Preparing and Using Glues

GLUING is frequently the most satisfactory method of fastening woodwork together. It is used almost to the exclusion of nails and screws in fine cabinet, furniture and pattern work. Glued joints between side and edge grain can be made stronger than the wood itself. Glue does not hold well on end grain, however, for it is drawn into the wood by the open cells of end grain before it has a chance to set.

The process of gluing consists essentially of applying liquid glue to the surfaces to be fastened together and then applying a clamping pressure which holds them together until the glue has set. It requires several hours for glue to set. Glue does not act as a cement and filler between two surfaces. Its holding power depends upon its bonding action. While in a liquid state, the glue penetrates the wood by passing into the tiny pores or spaces between the fibers. When the glue hardens, thousands of tiny filaments of glue reaching out between the wood fibers and clinging there join the two pieces of wood firmly together.

There is much more involved in the use of glue than spreading it on a joint and pressing the parts together. To make a strong joint requires knowledge and experience. Most of the necessary knowledge can be obtained by careful study of this chapter. Experience can be acquired by practice.

In mass production woodworking plants part or all of the gluing process is done by machinery. The glue is applied to the wood by glue-spreading machines and the parts are clamped together in special fixtures or presses. In small shops and schools and in the household, gluing is a hand operation. The glue is spread on the wood with a brush or small wooden paddle and the joints are pressed together with hand screws and clamps.

There are several kinds of glue, the common ones being fish, vegetable, animal, casein and plastic resin glues. Each of these has special properties and no one kind meets all requirements. It is necessary to choose the glue best suited to

165

the job to be done. Fish and vegetable glues are usually
liquid glues used cold and can generally be ignored by the
woodworker. The most useful glues in woodworking are the
animal, casein and plastic resin glues.

Prepared Liquid Glue. The glues which make the strong-
est and most enduring joints in wood are not sold in liquid
form and must be prepared when needed. There are many
brands of prepared liquid glues on the market which are
convenient to use and satisfactory for some purposes. Because they are ready to use immediately, they are good
household glues, handy when making minor quick repairs.
Their disadvantages are that they are not moistureproof
and they deteriorate with age.

Animal Glue. This was long the favorite glue of cabinetmakers but casein glue is gradually replacing it. Animal
glue is strong, sets quickly, flows into joints well and is stain-
less. Its disadvantages are that it requires time and care
in its preparation, must be used while hot and applied
quickly. It is satisfactory only for indoor work which is not
exposed to extreme moisture or mold-producing conditions.

Animal glue is made from hides, bones and other parts
of animals obtained from tanneries and slaughterhouses.
It reaches the retail market in sheet or flake form. Sheet
glue is very hard and brittle. The first step in preparing
it for use is to place it in a cloth or bag and break it into
small pieces with a hammer or mallet. The cloth or bag
will prevent the pieces from scattering.

A suitable glue pot is necessary for heating and melting
animal glue. A glue pot is always provided with a water
jacket so that the glue cannot be heated above 150 degrees
F. Use care not to boil glue. Heating above 150 degrees
F. weakens it. There are various glue pots on the market.
An electric glue pot is perhaps best but an ordinary double
boiler is satisfactory. Agateware is preferable to aluminum
for this purpose. When only a small quantity of glue is
needed, a tin can set in a pan of water may be used as a
glue pot.

Flake glue or small pieces of sheet glue are put in the
pot, covered with water and allowed to soak 12 to 16 hours.
Good grade glue is transparent and brittle before soaking.
After sufficient soaking the pieces will have swollen to several

times their original size, will become soft and jelly-like and will have absorbed most or all of the water. Then melt the glue by heating the double boiler on a gas stove or hot plate.

The proper amount of water in preparing animal glue varies with the glue and the kind of wood to be joined. It is usually

       glue 1 part   water 1 1/2 to 2 parts

by weight. The "rough" rule is usually 2 parts of water for hardwoods and 1 1/2 parts of water for softwoods. Continued or repeated heating of glue evaporates some of the water it contains, decreasing its strength. Inexperienced workmen usually make glue too thick. Thick glue prevents the parts of a joint from making the close contact which is necessary to secure strength. Hot animal glue should be thin enough to run freely from the brush. If it is too thick, add water.

Casein Glue. This glue is in wide use in woodworking plants. The amateur craftsman will find it superior to liquid and animal glues for home repairs and many other purposes. While not waterproof, casein glue is much more resistant to moisture and heat than animal glue. The latter must be applied quickly while it is hot. It sets rapidly. Not much speed is necessary in using casein glue, because it is used cold and does not begin to set until 10 to 15 minutes after application.

Casein glue is not satisfactory for work exposed to extreme moisture or mold-producing conditions. Under such circumstances a plastic resin glue should be used. Ordinary casein glue will stain certain kinds of wood, especially mahogany, oak and red wood. In fine cabinet work where glue stains would be objectionable, a special non-stain casein glue should be used.

Directions for mixing casein glue should be followed carefully. Put the required amount of *cold* water (50 to 70 degrees F.) in any convenient mixing cup or jar. Water below 50 degrees F. will make too thick a glue. Water above 70 degrees F. forms a glue which is too thin and sets too quickly. Add the dry casein glue powder to the water and stir rapidly for several seconds. The mixture will thicken and become pasty but do not add more water. The correct proportions of powder and water to use in making a mix are

1 part glue powder by volume (measure loosely filled)
1 part water by volume
      or
1 part glue powder by weight
2 parts cold water by weight

In other words mix one tablespoonful of glue powder with one tablespoonful of cold water or one ounce of dry powder with two ounces of water. Four ounces of dry glue mixed with 8 ounces of cold water will make from 3/4 to 1 pint of liquid glue.

When mixing the powder with water stir only until the powder has absorbed the water. Then let the mixture stand for 10 to 15 minutes. Stir again for a few seconds until smooth. Then the glue is ready to use.

The liquid life of casein glue mixed with water is not over 6 to 8 hours at 70 degrees F. Before the glue hardens, brushes and utensils which were used in gluing should be washed clean.

Plastic Resin Glues. These completely waterproof glues are sold under various trade names of which Cascamite and Weldwood are examples. Plastic resin glues are used for making wood joints which are to be exposed to water, weather and excessive dampness. They can be employed in boat-building. In most instances plastic resin glues set up hard enough to work in 4 to 8 hours but require 2 to 7 days to develop full strength and become waterproof.

Plastic resin glues reach the market in the form of dry powder and must be mixed with cold water before use. Directions for mixing are given on the container and it is essential to follow them closely. In general, the mixture of glue and water should have the consistency of heavy cream but should be applied to surfaces in a very *thin* spread only. The manufacturers of plastic resin glues supply pamphlets giving complete directions for mixing and using their product. It is advisable to obtain one from a hardware dealer or from the manufacturer.

Mix only as much resin glue as you need immediately. It will not remain a liquid for more than a few hours. Stir until all the water is absorbed and the mixture is smooth. It is then ready to use. Wash out brushes, spoons and uten-

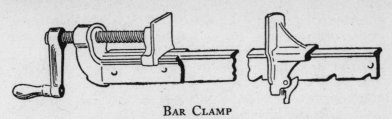

BAR CLAMP

sils in water soon after use before the glue has set.

The resin powder and the water for a mix may be measured by weight or by volume. The weight method is more satisfactory because it is more accurate. When measuring by volume do not pack or shake the powder down in the measure. Measure it loosely packed, just as it comes from the can. When measuring by volume use 2 parts of powder (loosely filled) to 1 part of cold water. The proper proportions by weight are 1 1/2 parts of powder and 1 part of cold water.

Pour one-half the measured water into a convenient mixing container. Add the measured glue powder and stir rapidly until the mixture is smooth. The glue is now ready to use. The remaining water can be discarded or all or part of it added to the mix. The amount of water controls the setting time of the glue. If you can work fast, use only one-half the water. This will make a stronger, faster-setting glue than if the whole amount were used.

The receptacle in which a plastic resin glue is mixed should be glass, china or enamelled ware free from all traces of alkali. Soda, soap and the residue of casein glues are alkaline and the presence of a slight trace in the mixing vessel will greatly retard the setting of a plastic resin glue.

General Directions for Gluing The conditions required for using the different glues vary. But there are two basic requirements which apply to all glues:

1. The joint must fit perfectly before glue is applied.
2. The glued surfaces must be pressed together and kept under pressure for several hours. This pressure time varies slightly with temperature, glue and type of wood. In general, soft woods should be kept under pressure for a minimum of 6 hours at 70 degrees F. and hardwoods for at least 8 hours at 70 degrees F.

All surfaces which are to be joined by glue *must fit together tightly*. When put under pressure they must touch at all points. Glue is not a space filler. It is true that if glue is thick enough, it will fill up a space in a joint, but *when it hardens it will crack* and the joint will not be strong. The adhesive strength which holds glue to wood is much greater than the cohesive strength which holds glue together. In other words, a thin film of glue between two pieces of wood makes a stronger job than a thick film.

It is advisable to test the fit of all pieces by clamping them together under pressure before applying any glue. If they do not fit perfectly, make them do so.

Clamps. Bar clamps, C clamps, handscrews, vises, heavy weights, rubber bands, wedges and cords are used to hold work together under pressure until the glue has set. Several clamps may be necessary to hold a job properly. It is sometimes necessary to make a special fixture to clamp irregular shapes and mitered joints. These are explained in a later paragraph.

Gluing Should Be a Planned Operation. To make a strong, permanent glued joint it is necessary to plan the whole operation. If it is a large job, it should be studied and divided into small units. This will make it easier to get the clamps in place quickly and true the joints. For example, it

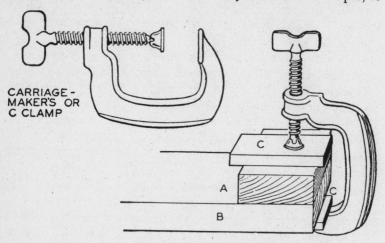

CARRIAGE-
MAKER'S OR
C CLAMP

USING THE C CLAMP

It is important to protect the work from being marred by the jaws of the clamp. A and B are clamped together. The two small pieces, marked C, protect A and B from being marred by the clamp. They are discarded when the glue has set and the clamp is removed.

would be difficult to glue together the back, front, side rails, legs and stretchers of a chair in one operation.

In addition to testing the fit of the parts to be glued, it is well to plan and test the method of clamping which is to be used. After the glue has been applied is the wrong time to discover that the handscrews or clamps slip or pull the work out of line. It may be necessary to prepare some small softwood blocks or strips which can be slipped between the clamps and finished surfaces to prevent the latter from being marred.

If a test proves the method of clamping to be satisfactory, all clamps and handscrews needed for the job should be adjusted so that they can be put back in place and tightened quickly and conveniently. Near at hand on the workbench should be a square, straight edge, rule, mallet, chisel, scraper

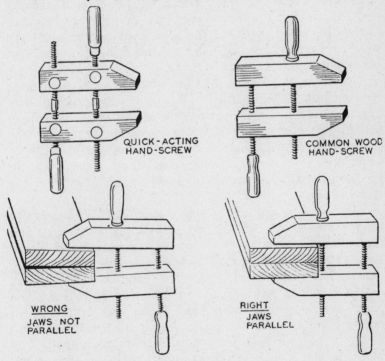

QUICK-ACTING HAND-SCREW

COMMON WOOD HAND-SCREW

WRONG
JAWS NOT PARALLEL

RIGHT
JAWS PARALLEL

Hand Screws

The jaws of this type of clamp must be parallel when tightened on the work or they may spring the work so that the surfaces to be glued do not meet properly.

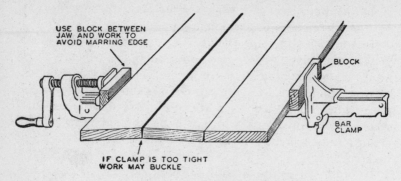

USE BLOCK BETWEEN
JAW AND WORK TO
AVOID MARRING EDGE

BLOCK

BAR
CLAMP

IF CLAMP IS TOO TIGHT
WORK MAY BUCKLE

USING THE BAR CLAMP
Too much clamping pressure may cause the work to buckle.

and a damp cloth. The square, straight edge and rule may be needed to check the alignment and squareness of the job when the clamping pressure is applied. Sometimes a tap with the mallet will help force the joint together or align the parts properly. The chisel, scraper and damp cloth are used for removing surplus glue before it hardens.

Directions for Using Animal Glue. Animal glue must be used hot. When chilled it does not penetrate into the pores of the wood and does not adhere satisfactorily. Also, chilled glue does not squeeze out of a joint properly when pressure is applied. Consequently the wood surfaces cannot come together. A weak joint results from the use of cold glue or glue which is too thick. It will come apart when the glue hardens and shrinks.

Speed is essential when using animal glue. Have everything ready so that no time is lost in applying the glue and the clamping pressure. The room temperature should not be less than 70 degrees F. It is well to warm the parts to be glued. The glue should be applied generously and quickly with a brush to the surfaces which are to be joined. The pieces are then immediately pressed together with sufficient pressure to squeeze all surplus glue out of the joint and bring the parts into close contact. With the clamps still in place the job should be checked for alignment, squareness, flatness, etc. Any necessary correction can then be made by shifting the position of the clamps and screws or adjusting the pressure. The joint must then remain clamped under pressure for several hours without disturbance.

Surplus glue which has been smeared on the work or squeezed out of the joint can be removed with a chisel or scraper as soon as it chills and thickens. If glue is removed while it is still warm, it will smear the surface. After it has thoroughly hardened, it is very difficult to cut off.

Directions for Using Casein Glue. Casein glue is used in much the same manner as animal glue. However, since casein glue is used cold and does not begin to set until 10 or 15 minutes after its application, room temperature and speed are not of quite as much importance.

The correct mixture of casein glue is much thicker than hot animal glue of the proper consistency. It should be applied in an even spread, preferably with a brush with very stiff bristles. Special brushes for applying casein glue can be purchased. Enough glue should be used so that it oozes out along the edges of the joint when the clamping pressure is applied. This surplus glue should be wiped off with a damp cloth immediately after the joint is clamped.

A job with casein glue should be planned so that the glue can be spread, pressure applied and the alignment of the parts checked (and corrected if necessary) within fifteen minutes. If too much time is taken, the glue may start to set and the excess will not squeeze out, preventing the parts from making proper contact. The room temperature preferably should not be below 70 degrees F. Softwood joints made with casein glue should be kept under strong pressure for at least 2 hours. Hardwood joints should be kept under pressure for a minimum of 4 hours and preferably 12 to 16 hours. Casein glue requires nearly a week to develop its full strength and water resistance. Do not strain or test casein joints until they have set for 7 days.

Some woods, among them teak, yellow pine, osage orange, lemonwood and yew are oily. Glue does not adhere to them as well as to other woods. Casein glue is the best glue to use for joining these materials. They can be improved for gluing by washing the surface with a strong solution of any alkaline household cleaning compound such as Gold Dust.

Directions for Using Plastic Resin Glue. When using plastic resin glues, the workroom and the material to be glued should be 70 degrees F. or warmer. The liquid life of a mix using three-quarters of the measure of water is 3 to 4 hours at 70 degrees F. Less water will shorten the liquid life, more water will lengthen it.

The joints to be glued must fit perfectly with no rough surfaces. Use a stiff brush to spread the glue and apply a film only about half as thick as is used with casein glue. Apply glue to *one surface only*. In other words, use much less plastic resin glue than casein or animal glues. There should be practically no oozing of glue from the joint when clamping pressure is applied.

Clamping pressure should be applied as soon as possible and continued for 5 hours at 70 degrees F. in the case of soft woods. Hard woods should be kept under pressure for 6 hours.

Plastic glues require nearly one week to develop full strength and water resistance. Joints made with this type of glue should not be strained until they have had full time to season.

Glue stains on exposed surfaces are objectionable in fine cabinet work. Even though the glue which is squeezed out of a joint when the clamps are applied is carefully wiped off it may leave stains. One of the tricks of cabinetmaking is to use a colored glue which will match the finish of the wood. Any glue which is prepared by mixing with water can be colored. All of the dry animal, casein or plastic resin glues can be colored. In the case of animal and casein glues this is done by dissolving water-soluble dye or alkali-proof dry earth color, obtainable at paint and hardware stores, in the water used for preparing the glue. The dye should be dissolved in the water before the glue powder is added. Plastic resin glues should be colored only with a soluble, *acid-fast* dye. No directions can be given as to how much dye should be used to produce any certain color. That must be ascertained by mixing some test samples. Very little dye is required. The tendency of the novice usually is to use too much.

Gluing Boards Edge to Edge. Butt joints between the edges of two boards can be made stronger and more permanent by gluing than by nailing or screwing together. Adjoining edges should be planed their entire length and fitted so that no cracks show on either side before the glue is

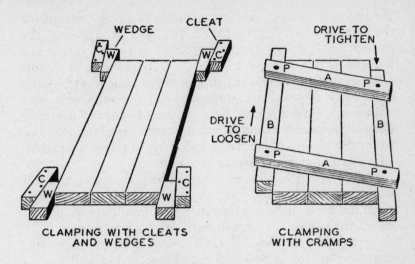

CLAMPING WITH CLEATS
AND WEDGES

CLAMPING
WITH CRAMPS

GLUING BOARDS EDGE TO EDGE

Wedges and cramps may be used in place of bar clamps. In the left-hand sketch, the blocks (C) are nailed to the workbench. Driving the wedges (W) between the blocks (C) and the boards clamps the boards together. The cramping method makes use of a frame composed of four strips A, A, B, B pivoted at the points marked P.

spread. If the pieces have been matched for figure and grain and carefully fitted, the glued joints will be practically invisible.

Some experienced craftsmen, after applying the glue, press the edges together and rub them back and forth several times before applying the clamps. There are many ways of clamping and holding boards together until the glue has set. Cabinetmakers' clamps, wedges, cleats and cramps may be used. Several of these are illustrated. The amateur craftsman who does not possess the equipment of a professional woodworker will find the cramping or cleat method most convenient. Regardless of the method of clamping, there is a tendency for long glued joints between edges to spring apart at the ends. Greater clamping pressure should be applied at the ends than in the center.

To glue two or more wide boards edge to edge, employ three clamps if cabinetmakers' or bar clamps are used. Place two of the clamps on the under side of the boards near opposite ends and the third clamp on the top side near the center. The center clamp should be tightened first, then the two end clamps. Avoid too much clamping pressure or the board may bulge in the center. Before applying the final pressure and putting the job away to set, test it for flatness with a straight-edge or framing square. The surfaces of the boards can be brought to the same level by holding a block of wood near the glue joint and tapping it with a mallet. In order for the finished work to form a perfectly flat surface as, for example, when boards are glued together to form a table top, it may be necessary to clamp a straight-edged board or plank *across* each end.

Gluing Doweled Joints. Cut a small V groove the full length of each dowel so that air and excess glue may escape when the dowel is forced into its hole. Point the end of each dowel slightly so that it will enter its hole more easily. In order to make a strong joint, all dowels must fit snugly into their corresponding holes. A simple method of building an under-sized dowel is described in the paragraph on gluing rickety chairs.

To Glue a Panel. If a panel is formed of more than one piece, the pieces should be glued together as described under **Gluing Boards Edge to Edge.** However, no glue should be

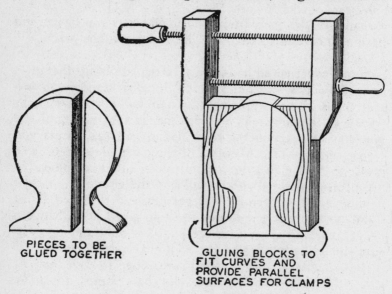

PIECES TO BE
GLUED TOGETHER

GLUING BLOCKS TO
FIT CURVES AND
PROVIDE PARALLEL
SURFACES FOR CLAMPS

SPECIAL GLUING BLOCKS ARE USED
ON CURVED AND IRREGULAR SHAPES

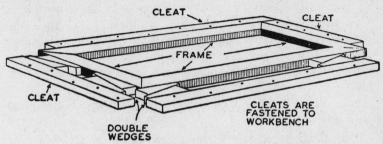

CLEAT CLEAT

FRAME

CLEAT

CLEATS ARE
FASTENED TO
WORKBENCH

DOUBLE
WEDGES

GLUING A MITERED FRAME REQUIRES A FIXTURE

The frame is laid on the workbench or a wide board. Four cleats are nailed to the workbench or board around the frame, leaving a short space at one side and one end between the frame and cleats. Double wedges made of wood are driven into the space between the cleats and frame to clamp the latter while the glue sets.

used to fasten the panel into the frame into which it fits. The panel itself should be free to expand and contract in accordance with changes in the moisture in the atmosphere.

To Glue Irregular Shapes. Clamps cannot be applied directly to some irregular shapes and curved surfaces. It is necessary to make special gluing blocks for them. The blocks are made to fit the curves and at the same time provide parallel surfaces for the jaws of the clamp so that the joint may be drawn up tightly. (See illustration.)

To Glue Miters. Pictures frames, mirrors and small panelled cabinet doors mitered at the corners cannot be drawn together with ordinary clamps. It is necessary to make a special fixture consisting of a board to which four cleats are fastened at right angles to each other. The mitered frame can be clamped together and the corners kept under pressure by driving double wedges between two of the cleats and the frame. (See illustration.) A piece of paper should be placed between each corner and the base of the fixture to prevent the glue squeezed out of the joints from fastening the frame to the fixture. Any paper which sticks to the frame can be removed with a sharp chisel and fine sandpaper.

Gluing Rickety Chairs and Furniture. One of the jobs which sometimes confronts the home craftsman is regluing a loose-jointed chair. The drying and consequent shrinkage which takes place in wood is the common cause of the loose joints which are found in rickety furniture.

No job of regluing a chair will prove satisfactory unless it is a thorough one. One or all of the rungs, legs and spindles of a wooden-bottomed chair may be loose. A single loose joint or a broken rung puts an undue strain on other joints and causes them to loosen. *All* loose joints must be reglued.

The job of regluing a chair must be planned. The correct procedure is:

1. Pull all loose joints apart and clean off all traces of old glue with a sharp chisel or penknife.

2. Put the chair together again and check all loose rungs, dowels, legs and spindles for fit. The joints must be tight. Dowels, rungs, legs and spindles should fit so tightly into their holes that they have to be driven into place with light taps from a mallet. Loose joints must be made to fit tightly before regluing.

3. Plan how best to apply the pressure necessary to draw all parts together and hold them in position. A combination of clamps, weights, heavy rubber bands and twisted cords may be necessary.

4. Take the chair apart and build up any loose joints so that they are a tight fit. When loose, the ends of rungs, legs and spindles can be made to fit tightly by wrapping with one or two layers of thin cotton cloth saturated with glue. A part thus built up should be left undisturbed for several hours, until the glue in the cloth has set.

A hole which is too large can often be built up and made smaller by using a crack filler made of glue, flour and sawdust as described elsewhere in this book.

5. Apply glue to the joints and assemble the chair. Drive all parts into place with a mallet, and put all joints under clamping pressure which will keep them drawn together. All clamping devices should remain in position for 24 hours. The chair should not be used or strained for several days so that the glue has opportunity to season and acquire its full strength.

Use casein or plastic resin glue when regluing a chair. These will make a stronger and more permanent job than ready-prepared liquid glues or animal glues. Remove all glue which squeezes out of the joints by wiping with a damp cloth as soon as the clamps are in place.

Parts of a chair which might b⸻
devices should be protected by ⸻
of cloth or paper. Strong rub⸻
secured by cutting strips fro⸻
Cords can be tightened s⸻
by slipping a short stick b⸻
tourniquet. The stick must ⸻
cannot untwist.

The procedure just described for ⸻
the correct one to use in regluing rickety⸻
other furniture.

How to Make Crack Filler. Woodworkers ha⸻
a mixture of fine sawdust and animal glue as a ⸻
small holes and cracks in wood. It is customary to us⸻
hogany sawdust for making filler for mahogany, pine sa⸻
dust for pine, etc. If woodwork is to be painted it makes
no difference what kind of sawdust is used. Sufficient sawdust should be thoroughly mixed with glue to produce a filler
having the consistency of thick paste. The filler must be
freshly prepared when needed. It soon hardens.

Since a filler of this type shrinks upon drying, fill cracks
and holes high enough to allow for shrinkage. Any excess
can be removed with fine sandpaper when it has dried.

A waterproof, stain-free, crack filler which is almost non-
shrinking can be made with plastic resin glue. Use the following formula and measure the ingredients by volume:

Dry plastic resin glue powder	1 part
White wheat or rye flour	1 part
Wood flour or very fine sawdust	1 part
Water	1 to 1 1/2 parts

Do not shake any of the dry ingredients down in the
measure; use them loosely packed. Use only common wheat
or rye flour—not the self-raising kind. Self-raising flours
contain chemicals which are injurious to plastic resin glues.

To prepare this type of filler, first mix all the dry ingredients together. Then add part of the water and stir until
it is completely absorbed. Add more water slowly and stir.
Use only enough water to make a mixture having the consistency of a very stiff paste.

Press the filler firmly into any cracks or holes to be filled.
Fill slightly higher than the level of the surrounding wood.

Remove ex⸻
This fille⸻
match th⸻
color th⸻

cess filler by sanding after it has dried overnight.
is very hard when dry. It can be stained to
e surrounding wood. Use only acid-fast dyes to
e filler.

Parts of a chair which might be marred by the clamping devices should be protected by wrapping with several layers of cloth or paper. Strong rubber bands for clamping can be secured by cutting strips from an old automobile inner tube. Cords can be tightened so as to exert considerable pressure by slipping a short stick between them and twisting like a tourniquet. The stick must be secured so that the cords cannot untwist.

The procedure just described for regluing a chair is also the correct one to use in regluing rickety tables, stands and other furniture.

How to Make Crack Filler. Woodworkers have long used a mixture of fine sawdust and animal glue as a filler for small holes and cracks in wood. It is customary to use mahogany sawdust for making filler for mahogany, pine sawdust for pine, etc. If woodwork is to be painted it makes no difference what kind of sawdust is used. Sufficient sawdust should be thoroughly mixed with glue to produce a filler having the consistency of thick paste. The filler must be freshly prepared when needed. It soon hardens.

Since a filler of this type shrinks upon drying, fill cracks and holes high enough to allow for shrinkage. Any excess can be removed with fine sandpaper when it has dried.

A waterproof, stain-free, crack filler which is almost non-shrinking can be made with plastic resin glue. Use the following formula and measure the ingredients by volume:

Dry plastic resin glue powder	1 part
White wheat or rye flour	1 part
Wood flour or very fine sawdust	1 part
Water	1 to 1 1/2 parts

Do not shake any of the dry ingredients down in the measure; use them loosely packed. Use only common wheat or rye flour—not the self-raising kind. Self-raising flours contain chemicals which are injurious to plastic resin glues.

To prepare this type of filler, first mix all the dry ingredients together. Then add part of the water and stir until it is completely absorbed. Add more water slowly and stir. Use only enough water to make a mixture having the consistency of a very stiff paste.

Press the filler firmly into any cracks or holes to be filled. Fill slightly higher than the level of the surrounding wood.

Remove excess filler by sanding after it has dried overnight. This filler is very hard when dry. It can be stained to match the surrounding wood. Use only acid-fast dyes to color the filler.

Index

Index